HISTORICAL FIGURES

DANIEL BOONE

THE PIONEER OF KENTUCKY

HISTORICAL FIGURES

Additional books and e-books in this series can be found on Nova's website under the Series tab.

HISTORICAL FIGURES

DANIEL BOONE

THE PIONEER OF KENTUCKY

JOHN S. C. ABBOTT

Copyright © 2019 by Nova Science Publishers, Inc.

All rights reserved. No part of this book may be reproduced, stored in a retrieval system or transmitted in any form or by any means: electronic, electrostatic, magnetic, tape, mechanical photocopying, recording or otherwise without the written permission of the Publisher.

We have partnered with Copyright Clearance Center to make it easy for you to obtain permissions to reuse content from this publication. Simply navigate to this publication's page on Nova's website and locate the "Get Permission" button below the title description. This button is linked directly to the title's permission page on copyright.com. Alternatively, you can visit copyright.com and search by title, ISBN, or ISSN.

For further questions about using the service on copyright.com, please contact:
Copyright Clearance Center
Phone: +1-(978) 750-8400   Fax: +1-(978) 750-4470   E-mail: info@copyright.com.

NOTICE TO THE READER

The Publisher has taken reasonable care in the preparation of this book, but makes no expressed or implied warranty of any kind and assumes no responsibility for any errors or omissions. No liability is assumed for incidental or consequential damages in connection with or arising out of information contained in this book. The Publisher shall not be liable for any special, consequential, or exemplary damages resulting, in whole or in part, from the readers' use of, or reliance upon, this material. Any parts of this book based on government reports are so indicated and copyright is claimed for those parts to the extent applicable to compilations of such works.

Independent verification should be sought for any data, advice or recommendations contained in this book. In addition, no responsibility is assumed by the Publisher for any injury and/or damage to persons or property arising from any methods, products, instructions, ideas or otherwise contained in this publication.

This publication is designed to provide accurate and authoritative information with regard to the subject matter covered herein. It is sold with the clear understanding that the Publisher is not engaged in rendering legal or any other professional services. If legal or any other expert assistance is required, the services of a competent person should be sought. FROM A DECLARATION OF PARTICIPANTS JOINTLY ADOPTED BY A COMMITTEE OF THE AMERICAN BAR ASSOCIATION AND A COMMITTEE OF PUBLISHERS.

Additional color graphics may be available in the e-book version of this book.

Library of Congress Cataloging-in-Publication Data

ISBN: 978-1-53616-030-7

Published by Nova Science Publishers, Inc. † New York

Contents

Preface		xiii
Chapter 1	The Discovery and early Settlement of America	1
Chapter 2	Daniel Boone, his Parentage, and Early Adventures	17
Chapter 3	Louisiana, Its Discovery and Vicissitudes	39
Chapter 4	Camp Life Beyond the Alleghanies	49
Chapter 5	Indian Warfare	61
Chapter 6	Sufferings of the Pioneers	73
Chapter 7	Life in the Wilderness	87
Chapter 8	Captivity and Flight	105
Chapter 9	Victories and Defeats	121
Chapter 10	British Allies	135
Chapter 11	Kentucky Organized as a State	147
Chapter 12	Adventures Romantic and Perilous	161
Chapter 13	A New Home	175

Chapter 14	Conclusion	**191**
Index		**199**
Related Nova Publications		**205**

"His youth was innocent; his riper age,
Marked with some act of goodness every day;
And watched by eyes that loved him, calm and sage,
Faded his late declining years away.
Cheerful he gave his being up and went
To share the holy rest that waits a life well spent."

New York:
Dodd & Mead, No. 762 Broadway.
1872.

PREFACE[*]

The name of Daniel Boone is a conspicuous one in the annals of our country. And yet there are but few who are familiar with the events of his wonderful career, or who have formed a correct estimate of the character of the man. Many suppose that he was a rough, coarse backwoodsman, almost as savage as the bears he pursued in the chase, or the Indians whose terrors he so perseveringly braved. Instead of this, he was one of the most mild and unboastful of men; feminine as a woman in his tastes and his deportment, never uttering a coarse word, never allowing himself in a rude action. He was truly one of nature's *gentle* men. With all this instinctive refinement and delicacy, there was a boldness of character which seemed absolutely incapable of experiencing the emotion of fear. And surely all the records of chivalry may be searched in vain for a career more full of peril and of wild adventure.

This narrative reveals a state of society and habitudes of life now rapidly passing into oblivion. It is very desirable that the record should be perpetuated, that we may know the scenes through which our fathers passed, in laying the foundations of this majestic Republic. It is probable

---

[*] This is an edited, augmented and reformatted version of "Daniel Boone: The Pioneer of Kentucky" by John S. C. Abbott, originally published by New York, Dodd & Mead, dated 1872. The views, opinions, and nomenclature expressed in this book are those of the authors and do not reflect the views of Nova Science Publishers, Inc.

that as the years roll on the events which occurred in the infancy of our nation will be read with ever-increasing interest.

It is the intention of the publisher of this volume to issue a series of sketches of the prominent men in the early history of our country. The next volume will contain the life and adventures of the renowned Miles Standish, the Puritan Captain.

John S. C. Abbott,
Fair Haven, Conn.

Chapter 1

THE DISCOVERY AND EARLY SETTLEMENT OF AMERICA

The little fleet of three small vessels, with which Columbus left Palos in Spain, in search of a new world, had been sixty-seven days at sea. They had traversed nearly three thousand miles of ocean, and yet there was nothing but a wide expanse of waters spread out before them. The despairing crew were loud in their murmurs, demanding that the expedition should be abandoned and that the ships should return to Spain. The morning of the 11th of October, 1492, had come. During the day Columbus, whose heart had been very heavily oppressed with anxiety, had been cheered by some indications that they were approaching land. Fresh seaweed was occasionally seen and a branch of a shrub with leaves and berries upon it, and a piece of wood curiously carved had been picked up.

The devout commander was so animated by these indications, that he gathered his crew around him and returned heartfelt thanks to God, for this prospect that their voyage would prove successful. It was a beautiful night, the moon shone brilliantly and a delicious tropical breeze swept the ocean. At ten o'clock Columbus stood upon the bows of his ship earnestly gazing upon the western horizon, hoping that the long-looked-for land would rise before him. Suddenly he was startled by the distinct gleam of a torch far off in the distance. For a moment it beamed forth with a clear and indisputable flame and then disappeared. The agitation of Columbus no words can describe. Was it a meteor? Was it an optical illusion? Was it light from the land?

Suddenly the torch, like a star, again shone forth with distinct though faint gleam. Columbus called some of his companions to his side and they also saw the light clearly. But again it disappeared. At two o'clock in the morning a sailor at the look out on the mast head shouted, "Land! land! land!" In a few moments all beheld, but a few miles distant from them, the distinct outline of towering mountains piercing the skies. A new world was discovered. Cautiously the vessels hove to and waited for the light of the morning. The dawn of day presented to the eyes of Columbus and his companions a spectacle of beauty which the garden of Eden could hardly have rivalled. It was a morning of the tropics, calm, serene and lovely. But two miles before them there emerged from the sea an island of mountains and valleys, luxuriant with every variety of tropical vegetation. The voyagers, weary of gazing for many weeks on the wide waste of waters, were so enchanted with the fairy scene which then met the eye, that they seemed really to believe that they had reached the realms of the blest.

The boats were lowered, and, as they were rowed towards the shore, the scene every moment grew more beautiful. Gigantic trees draped in luxuriance of foliage hitherto unimagined, rose in the soft valleys and upon the towering hills. In the sheltered groves, screened from the sun, the picturesque dwellings of the natives were thickly clustered. Flowers of every variety of tint bloomed in marvelous profusion. The trees seemed laden with fruits of every kind, and in inexhaustible abundance. Thousands of natives crowded the shore, whose graceful forms and exquisitely moulded limbs indicated the innocence and simplicity of Eden before the fall.

Columbus, richly attired in a scarlet dress, fell upon his knees as he reached the beach, and, with clasped hands and uplifted eyes, gave utterance to the devout feelings which ever inspired him, in thanksgiving to God. In recognition of the divine protection he gave the island the name of San Salvador, or Holy Savior. Though the new world thus discovered was one of the smallest islands of the Caribbean Sea, no conception was then formed of the vast continents of North and South America, stretching out in both directions, for many leagues almost to the Arctic and Antarctic poles.

Omitting a description of the wonderful adventures which ensued, we can only mention that two years after this, the southern extremity of the North American continent was discovered by Sebastian Cabot. It was in the spring of the year and the whole surface of the soil seemed carpeted with the most brilliant flowers. The country consequently received the beautiful name of Florida. It, of course, had no boundaries, for no one knew with certainty whether it were an island or a continent, or how far its limits might extend.

The years rolled on and gradually exploring excursions crept along the coast towards the north, various provinces were mapped out with pretty distinct boundaries upon the Atlantic coast, extending indefinitely into the vast and unknown interior. Expeditions from France had entered the St. Lawrence and established settlements in Canada. For a time the whole Atlantic coast, from its extreme southern point to Canada, was called Florida. In the year 1539, Ferdinand De Soto, an unprincipled Spanish warrior, who had obtained renown by the conquest of Peru in South America, fitted out by permission of the king of Spain, an expedition of nearly a thousand men to conquer and take possession of that vast and indefinite realm called Florida.

We have no space here to enter upon a description of the fiendlike cruelties practiced by these Spaniards. They robbed and enslaved without mercy. In pursuit of gold they wandered as far north as the present boundary of South Carolina. Then turning to the west, they traversed the vast region to the Mississippi river. The forests were full of game. The granaries of the simple-hearted natives were well stored with corn; vast prairies spreading in all directions around them, waving with grass and blooming with flowers, presented ample forage for the three hundred horses which accompanied the expedition. They were also provided with fierce bloodhounds to hunt down the terrified natives. Thus invincible and armed with the "thunder and lightning" of their guns, they swept the country, perpetrating every conceivable outrage upon the helpless natives.

After long and unavailing wanderings in search of gold, having lost by sickness and the casualties of such an expedition nearly half their number, the remainder built boats upon the Mississippi, descended that rapid stream five hundred miles to its mouth, and then skirting the coast of Texas, finally disappeared on the plains of Mexico. De Soto, the leader of this conquering band, died miserably on the Mississippi, and was buried beneath its waves.

The whole country which these adventurers traversed, they found to be quite densely populated with numerous small tribes of natives, each generally wandering within circumscribed limits. Though these tribes spoke different languages, or perhaps different dialects of the same language, they were essentially the same in appearance, manners and customs. They were of a dark-red color, well-formed and always disposed to receive the pale face strangers with kindliness, until exasperated by ill-treatment. They lived in fragile huts called wigwams, so simple in their structure that one could easily be erected in a few hours. These huts were generally formed by setting long and slender poles in the ground, inclosing an area of from ten to eighteen feet in diameter, according to the size of the family. The tops were tied together, leaving a hole for the escape of smoke from the central fire. The sides were thatched with coarse grass, or so covered with the bark of trees, as quite effectually to exclude both wind and rain. There were no windows, light entering only through the almost always open door. The ground floor was covered with dried grass, or the skins of animals, or with the soft and fragrant twigs of some evergreen tree.

The inmates, men, women and children, seated upon these cushions, presented a very attractive and cheerful aspect. Several hundred of these wigwams were frequently clustered upon some soft meadow by the side of a flowing stream, fringed with a gigantic forest, and exhibited a spectacle of picturesque loveliness quite charming to the beholder. The furniture of these humble abodes was extremely simple. They had no pots or kettles which would stand the fire. They had no knives nor forks; no tables nor chairs. Sharp flints, such as they could find served for knives, with which, with incredible labor, they sawed down small trees and fashioned their bows and arrows. They had no roads except foot paths through the wilderness, which for generations their ancestors had traversed, called "trails." They had no beasts of burden, no cows, no flocks nor herds of any kind. They generally had not even salt, but cured their meat by drying it in the sun. They had no ploughs, hoes, spades, consequently they could only cultivate the lightest soil. With a sharp stick, women loosened the earth, and then depositing their corn or maize, cultivated it in the rudest manner.

These Indians acquired the reputation of being very faithful friends, but very bitter enemies. It was said they never forgot a favor, and never forgave an insult. They were cunning rather than brave. It was seldom that an Indian could be induced to meet a foe in an open hand-to-hand fight. But he would track him for years, hoping to take him unawares and to brain him with the tomahawk, or pierce his heart with the flint-pointed arrow.

About the year 1565, a company of French Protestants repaired to Florida, hoping there to find the liberty to worship God in accordance with their interpretation of the teachings of the Bible. They established quite a flourishing colony, at a place which they named St. Marys, near the coast. This was the first European settlement on the continent of North America. The fanatic Spaniards, learning that Protestants had taken possession of the country, sent out an expedition and utterly annihilated the settlement, putting men, women and children to the sword. Many of these unfortunate Protestants were hung in chains from trees under the inscription, "*Not as Frenchmen but as Heretics.*" The blood-stained Spaniards then established themselves at a spot nearby, which they called St. Augustine. A French gentleman of wealth fitted out a well-manned and well-armed expedition of three ships, attacked the murderers by surprise and put them to death. Several corpses were suspended from trees, under the inscription, "*Not as Spaniards, but as Murderers.*"

There was an understanding among the powers of Europe, that any portion of the New World discovered by expeditions from European courts, should be recognised as belonging to that court. The Spaniards had taken possession in Florida. Far away a thousand leagues to the North, the French had entered the gulf of St. Lawrence. But little was known of the vast region between. A young English gentleman, Sir Walter Raleigh, an earnest Protestant, and one who had fought with the French Protestants in their religious wars, roused by the massacre of his friends in Florida, applied to the British court to fit out a colony to take possession of the intermediate country. He hoped thus to prevent the Spanish monarchy, and the equally intolerant French court, from spreading their principles over the whole continent. The Protestant Queen Elizabeth then occupied the throne of Great Britain. Raleigh was young, rich, handsome and marvelously fascinating in his address. He became a great favorite of the maiden queen, and she gave him a commission, making him lord of all the continent of North America, between Florida and Canada.

The whole of this vast region without any accurate boundaries, was called Virginia. Several ships were sent to explore the country. They reached the coast of what is now called North Carolina, and the adventurers landed at Roanoke Island. They were charmed with the climate, with the friendliness of the natives and with the majestic growth of the forest trees, far surpassing anything they had witnessed in the Old World. Grapes in rich clusters hung in profusion on the vines, and birds of every variety of song and plumage filled the groves. The expedition returned to England with such glowing accounts of the realm they had discovered, that seven ships were fitted out, conveying one hundred and eight men, to colonise the island. It is quite remarkable that no women accompanied the expedition. Many of these men were reckless adventurers. Bitter hostility soon sprang up between them and the Indians, who at first had received them with the greatest kindness.

Most of these colonists were men unaccustomed to work, and who insanely expected that in the New World, in some unknown way, wealth was to flow in upon them like a flood. Disheartened, homesick and appalled by the hostile attitude which the much oppressed Indians were beginning to assume, they were all anxious to return home. When, soon after, some ships came bringing them abundant supplies, they with one accord abandoned the colony, and crowding the vessels returned to England. Fifteen men however consented to remain, to await the arrival of fresh colonists from the Mother Country.

Sir Walter Raleigh, still undiscouraged, in the next year 1587 sent out another fleet containing a number of families as emigrants, with women and children. When they arrived, they found Roanoke deserted. The fifteen men had been murdered by the Indians in retaliation for the murder of their chief and several of his warriors by the English. With fear and trembling the new settlers decided to remain, urging the friends who had accompanied them to hasten back to England with the ships and bring them reinforcements and supplies. Scarcely had they spread their sails on the return voyage ere war broke out with Spain. It was three years before another ship crossed the ocean, to see what had become of the colony. It had utterly disappeared. Though many attempts were made to ascertain its tragic fate, all were unavailing. It is probable that many were put to death by the Indians, and perhaps the children were carried far back into the interior and incorporated into their tribes. This bitter disappointment seemed to paralyse the energies of colonization. For more than seventy years the Carolinas remained a wilderness, with no attempt to transfer to them the civilization of the Old World. Still English ships continued occasionally to visit the coast. Some came to fish, some to purchase furs of the Indians, and some for timber for shipbuilding. The stories which these voyagers told on their return, kept up an interest in the New World. It was indeed an attractive picture which could be truthfully painted. The climate was mild, genial and salubrious. The atmosphere surpassed the far-famed transparency of Italian skies. The forests were of gigantic growth, more picturesquely beautiful than any ever planted by man's hand, and they were filled with game. The lakes and streams swarmed with fish. A wilderness of flowers, of every variety of loveliness, bloomed over the wide meadows and the broad savannahs, which the forest had not yet invaded. Berries and fruits were abundant. In many places the soil was surpassingly rich, and easily tilled; and all this was open, without money and without price, to the first comer.

Still more than a hundred years elapsed after the discovery of these realms, ere any permanent settlement was effected upon them. Most of the bays, harbors and rivers were unexplored, and reposed as it were in the solemn silence of eternity. From the everglades of Florida to the firclad hills of Nova Scotia, not a settlement of white men could be found.

At length in the year 1607, a number of wealthy gentlemen in London formed a company to make a new attempt for the settlement of America. It was their plan to send out hardy colonists, abundantly provided with arms, tools and provisions. King James I., who had succeeded his cousin Queen Elizabeth, granted them a charter, by which, wherever they might effect a landing, they were to be the undisputed lords of a territory extending a hundred miles along the coast, and running back one hundred miles into the interior. Soon after, a similar grant was conferred upon another association, for the region of North Virginia, now called New England.

Under the protection of this London Company, one hundred and five men, with no women or children, embarked in three small ships for the Southern Atlantic coast of North America. Apparently by accident, they entered Chesapeake Bay, where they found a broad and deep stream, which they named after their sovereign, James River. As they ascended this beautiful stream, they were charmed with the loveliness which nature had spread so profusely around them. Upon the northern banks of the river, about fifty miles from its entrance into the bay, they selected a spot for their settlement, which they named Jamestown. Here they commenced cutting down trees and raising their huts.

In an enterprise of this kind, muscles inured to work and determined spirits ready to grapple with difficulties, are essential. In such labors, the most useless of all beings is the gentleman with soft hands and luxurious habits. Unfortunately quite a number of pampered sons of wealth had joined the colony. Being indolent, selfish and dissolute, they could do absolutely nothing for the prosperity of the settlement, but were only an obstacle in the way of its growth.

Troubles soon began to multiply, and but for the energies of a remarkable man, Capt. John Smith, the colony must soon have perished through anarchy. But even Capt. John Smith with all his commanding powers, and love of justice and of law, could not prevent the idle and profligate young men from insulting the natives, and robbing them of their corn. With the autumnal rains sickness came, and many died. The hand of well-organised industry might have raised an ample supply of corn to meet all their wants through the short winter. But this had been neglected, and famine was added to sickness, Capt. Smith had so won the confidence of the Indian chieftains, that notwithstanding the gross irregularities of his young men, they brought him supplies of corn and game, which they freely gave to the English in their destitution.

Captain Smith having thus provided for the necessities of the greatly diminished colony, set out with a small party of men on an exploring expedition into the interior. He was waylayed by Indians, who with arrows and tomahawks speedily put all the men to death, excepting the leader, who was taken captive. There was something in the demeanor of this brave man which overawed them. He showed them his pocket compass, upon which they gazed with wonder. He then told them that if they would send to the fort a leaf from his pocket-book, upon which he had made several marks with his pencil, they would find the next day, at any spot they might designate, a certain number of axes, blankets, and other articles of great value to them. Their curiosity was exceedingly aroused; the paper was sent, and the next day the articles were found as promised. The Indians looked upon Captain Smith as a magician, and treated him with great respect. Still the more thoughtful of the natives regarded him as a more formidable foe. They could not be blind to the vastly superior power of the English in their majestic ships, with their long swords, and terrible fire-arms, and all the developments, astounding to them, of a higher civilization. They were very anxious in view of encroachments which might eventually give the English the supremacy in their land.

Powhatan, the king of the powerful tribe who had at first been very friendly to the English, summoned a council of war of his chieftains, and after long deliberation, it was decided that Captain Smith was too powerful a man to be allowed to live, and that he must die. He was accordingly led out to execution, but without any of the ordinary accompaniments of torture. His hands were bound behind him, he was laid upon the ground, and his head was placed upon a stone. An Indian warrior of herculean strength stood by, with a massive club, to give the death blow by crushing in the skull. Just as the fatal stroke was about to descend, a beautiful Indian girl, Pocahontas, the daughter of the king, rushed forward and throwing her arms around the neck of Captain Smith, placed her head upon his. The Indians regarded this as an indication from the Great Spirit that the life of Captain Smith was to be spared, and they set their prisoner at liberty, who, being thus miraculously rescued, returned to Jamestown.

By his wisdom Captain Smith preserved for some time friendly relations with the Indians, and the colony rapidly increased, until there were five hundred Europeans assembled at Jamestown. Capt. Smith being severely wounded by an accidental explosion of gunpowder, returned to England for surgical aid. The colony, thus divested of his vigorous sway, speedily lapsed into anarchy. The bitter hostility of the Indians was aroused, and, within a few months, the colony dwindled away beneath the ravages of sickness, famine, and the arrows of the Indians, to but sixty men. Despair reigned in all hearts, and this starving remnant of Europeans was preparing to abandon the colony and return to the Old World, when Lord Delaware arrived with several ships loaded with provisions and with a reinforcement of hardy laborers. Most of the idle and profligate young men who had brought such calamity upon the colony, had died. Those who remained took fresh courage, and affairs began to be more prosperous.

The organization of the colony had thus far been effected with very little regard to the wants of human nature. There were no women there. Without the honored wife there cannot be the happy home; and without the home there can be no contentment. To herd together five hundred men upon the banks of a foreign stream, three thousand miles from their native land, without women and children, and to expect them to lay the foundation of a happy and prosperous colony, seems almost unpardonable folly.

Emigrants began to arrive with their families, and in the year 1620, one hundred and fifty poor, but virtuous young women, were induced to join the Company. Each young man who came received one hundred acres of land. Eagerly these young planters, in short courtship, selected wives from such of these women as they could induce to listen to them. Each man paid one hundred and fifty pounds of tobacco to defray the expenses of his wife's voyage. But the wickedness of man will everywhere, and under all circumstances, make fearful development of its power. Many desperadoes joined the colony. The poor Indians with no weapons of war but arrows, clubs and stone tomahawks, were quite at the mercy of the English with their keen swords, and death-dealing muskets. Fifteen Europeans could easily drive several hundred Indians in panic over the plains. Unprincipled men perpetrated the grossest outrages upon the families of the Indians, often insulting the proudest chiefs.

The colonists were taking up lands in all directions. Before their unerring rifles, game was rapidly disappearing. The Indians became fully awake to their danger. The chiefs met in council, and a conspiracy was formed, to put, at an appointed hour, all the English to death, every man, woman and child. Every house was marked. Two or three Indians were appointed to make the massacre sure in each dwelling. They were to spread over the settlement, enter the widely scattered log-huts, as friends, and at a certain moment were to spring upon their unsuspecting victims, and kill them instantly. The plot was fearfully successful in all the dwellings outside the little village of Jamestown. In one hour, on the 22nd of March, 1622, three hundred and forty-seven men, women and children were massacred in cold blood. The colony would have been annihilated, but for a Christian Indian who, just before the massacre commenced, gave warning to a friend in Jamestown. The Europeans rallied with their firearms, and easily drove off their foes, and then commenced the unrelenting extermination of the Indians. An arrow can be thrown a few hundred feet, a musket ball more than as many yards. The Indians were consequently helpless. The English shot down both sexes, young and old, as mercilessly as if they had been wolves. They seized their houses, their lands, their pleasant villages. The Indians were either slain or driven far away from the houses of their fathers, into the remote wilderness.

The colony now increased rapidly, and the cabins of the emigrants spread farther and farther over the unoccupied lands. These hardy adventurers seemed providentially imbued with the spirit of enterprise. Instead of clustering together for the pleasure of society and for mutual protection, they were ever pushing into the wild and unknown interior, rearing their cabins on the banks of distant streams, and establishing their silent homes in the wildest solitudes of the wilderness. In 1660, quite a number of emigrants moved directly south from Virginia, to the river Chowan, in what is now South Carolina, where they established a settlement which they called Albermarle. In 1670, a colony from England established itself at Charleston, South Carolina. Thus gradually the Atlantic coast became fringed with colonies, extending but a few leagues back into the country from the sea-shore, while the vast interior remained an unexplored wilderness. As the years rolled on, ship-loads of emigrants arrived, new settlements were established, colonial States rose into being, and, though there were many sanguinary conflicts with the Indians, the Europeans were always in the end triumphant, and intelligence, wealth, and laws of civilization were rapidly extended along the Atlantic border of the New World.

For many years there had been a gradual pressure of the colonists towards the west, steadily encroaching upon the apparently limitless wilderness. To us it seems strange that they did not, for the sake of protection against the Indians, invariably go in military bands. But generally this was not the case. The emigrants seem to have been inspired with a spirit of almost reckless indifference to danger; they apparently loved the solitude of the forest, avoided neighbors who might interfere with their hunting and trapping, and reared their humble cottages in the wildest ravines of the mountains and upon the smooth meadows which border the most solitary streams; thus gradually the tide of emigration, flowing through Indian trails and along the forest-covered vines, was approaching the base of the Alleghany mountains.

But little was known of the character of the boundless realms beyond the ridges of this gigantic chain. Occasionally a wandering Indian who had chased his game over those remote wilds, would endeavor to draw upon the sand, with a stick, a map of the country showing the flow of the rivers, the line of the mountains, and the sweep of the open prairies. The Ohio was then called the Wabash. This magnificent and beautiful stream is formed by the confluence of the Alleghany and the Monongahela rivers. It was a long voyage, a voyage of several hundred miles, following the windings of the Monongahela River from its rise among the mountains of Western

Virginia till, far away in the north, it met the flood of the Alleghany, at the present site of the city of Pittsburg. The voyage, in a birch canoe, required, in the figurative language of the Indians, "two paddles, two warriors and three moons."

The Indians very correctly described the Ohio, or the Wabash, as but the tributary of a much more majestic stream, far away in the west, which, pouring its flood through the impenetrable forest, emptied itself they knew not where. Of the magnitude of this distant river, the Mississippi, its source, rise and termination, they could give no intelligible account. They endeavored to give some idea of the amount of game to be found in those remote realms, by pointing to the leaves of the forest and the stars in the sky.

The settlers were deeply interested and often much excited by the glowing descriptions thus given them of a terrestrial Eden, where life would seem to be but one uninterrupted holiday. Occasionally an adventurous French or Spanish trader would cross the towering mountains and penetrate the vales beyond. They vied with the Indians in their account of the salubrity of the climate, the brilliance of the skies, the grandeur of the forests, the magnificence of the rivers, the marvelous fertility of the soil and the abundance of game.

As early as the year 1690 a trader from Virginia, by the name of Doherty, crossed the mountains, visited the friendly Cherokee nation, within the present bounds of Georgia, and resided with the natives several years. In the year 1730 an enterprising and intelligent man from South Carolina, by the name of Adair, took quite an extensive tour through most of the villages of the Cherokees, and also visited several tribes south and west of them. He wrote an exceedingly valuable and interesting account of his travels which was published in London.

Influenced by these examples several traders, in the year 1740, went from Virginia to the country of the Cherokees. They carried on pack horses goods which the Indians valued, and which they exchanged for furs, which were sold in Europe at an enormous profit.

A hatchet, a knife, a trap, a string of beads, which could be bought for a very small sum in the Atlantic towns, when exhibited beyond the mountains to admiring groups in the wigwam of the Indian, could be exchanged for furs which were of almost priceless value in the metropolitan cities of the Old World. This traffic was mutually advantageous, and so long as peaceful relations existed between the white man and the Indian, was prosecuted with great and ever increasing vigor. The Indians thus obtained the steel trap, the keenly cutting ax, and the rifle, which he soon learned to use with unerring aim. He was thus able in a day to obtain more game than with his arrows and his clumsy snares he could secure in a month.

This friendly intercourse was in all respects very desirable; and but for the depravity of the white man it might have continued uninterrupted for generations. But profligate and vagabond adventurers from the settlements defrauded the Indians, insulted their women, and often committed wanton murder. But it would seem that the majority of the traders were honest men. Ramsay, in his Annals of Tennessee, writes, in reference to this traffic:

> "Other advantages resulted from it to the whites. They became thus acquainted with the great avenues leading through the hunting ground, and to the occupied country of the neighboring tribes—an important circumstance in the condition of either peace or war. Further the traders were an exact thermometer of the pacific or hostile intention and feelings of the Indians with whom they traded. Generally they were foreigners, most frequently Scotchmen, who had not been long in the country, or upon the frontier; who, having experienced none of the cruelties, depredations or aggressions of the Indians, cherished none of the resentment and spirit of retaliation born with and everywhere manifested by the American settler.
>
> "Thus free from animosity against the aborigines, the trader was allowed to remain in the village, where he traded, unmolested, even where its warriors were singing the war song or brandishing the war club, preparatory to an invasion or massacre of the whites. Timely warning was thus often given by a returning packman to a feeble and unsuspecting settlement, of the perfidy and cruelty meditated against it."

Game on the eastern side of the Alleghanies, hunted down alike by white men and Indians, soon became scarce. Adventurers combining the characters of traders and hunters rapidly multiplied. Many of the hunters among the white men far outstripped the Indians in skill and energy. Thus some degree of jealousy was excited on the part of the savages. They saw how rapidly the game was disappearing, and these thoughtful men began to be anxious for the future. With no love for agriculture the destruction of the game was their ruin.

As early as the year 1748 quite a party of gentlemen explorers, under the leadership of Doctor Thomas Walker of Virginia, crossed a range of the Alleghany Mountains, which the Indians called Warioto, but to which Doctor Walker gave the name of Cumberland, in honor of the Duke of Cumberland who was then prime minister of England. Following along this chain in a south-westerly direction, in search of some pass or defile by which they could cross the cliffs, they came to the remarkable depression in the mountains to which they gave the name of Cumberland Gap. On the western side of the range they found a beautiful mountain stream, rushing far away, with ever increasing volume, into the unknown wilderness, which the Indians called Shawnee, but which Doctor Walker's party baptised with the name of Cumberland River. These names have adhered to the localities upon which they were thus placed.

In 1756 a feeble attempt was made to establish a colony upon the Tennessee River, at a spot which was called London. This was one hundred and fifty miles in advance of any white settlement. Eight years passed, and by the ravages of war the little settlement went up in flame and smoke. As the years rapidly came and went there were occasional bursts of the tempests of war; again there would be a short lull and blessed peace would come with its prosperity and joy.

"In the year 1760, Doctor Walker again passed over Clinch and Powell's rivers on a tour of exploration, into what is now Kentucky. The Cherokees were then at peace with the whites, and hunters from the back settlements began, with safety, to penetrate deeper and further into the wilderness of Tennessee. Several of them, chiefly from Virginia, hearing of the abundance of game with which the woods were stocked, and allured by the prospect of gain which might be drawn from this source, formed themselves into a company composed of Wallen, Seagys, Blevins, Cox and fifteen others, and came into the valley, since known as Carter's Valley, in Hawkin's county, Tennessee. They hunted eighteen months upon Clinch and Powell rivers. Wallen's Creek and Wallen's Ridge received their name from the leader of the company; as also did Wallen's Station which they erected in the Lee county, Virginia.

"They penetrated as far north as Laurel Mountain, in Kentucky, where they terminated their journey, having met with a body of Indians whom they supposed to be Shawnees. At the head of one of the companies that visited the West, this year, came Daniel Boone from the Yadkin, in North Carolina, and travelled with them as low as the place where Abingdon now stands, and there left them."

This is the first time the advent of Daniel Boone to the western wilds has been mentioned by historians or by the several biographers of that distinguished pioneer and hunter. There is reason however to believe that he hunted upon Watauga some time earlier than this.

Chapter 2

DANIEL BOONE, HIS PARENTAGE, AND EARLY ADVENTURES

It was but a narrow fringe upon the sea coast of North America, which was thus far occupied by the European emigrants. Even this edge of the continent was so vast in its extent, from the southern capes of Florida to the gulf of St. Lawrence, that these colonial settlements were far separated from each other. They constituted but little dots in the interminable forest: the surges of the Atlantic beating upon their eastern shores, and the majestic wilderness sweeping in its sublime solitude behind them on the west. Here the painted Indians pursued their game, while watching anxiously the encroachments of the pale faces. The cry of the panther, the growling of the bear, and the howling of the wolf, were music to the settlers compared with the war-hoop of the savage, which often startled the inmates of the lonely cabins, and consigned them to that sleep from which there is no earthly waking. The Indians were generally hostile, and being untutored savages, they were as merciless as demons in their revenge. The mind recoils from the contemplation of the tortures to which they often exposed their captives. And one cannot but wonder that the Almighty Father could have allowed such agony to be inflicted upon any of His creatures.

Notwithstanding the general desire of the colonial authorities to treat the Indians with justice and kindness, there were unprincipled adventurers crowding all the colonies, whose wickedness no laws could restrain. They robbed the Indians, insulted their families, and inflicted upon them outrages which goaded the poor savages to desperation. In their unintelligent vengeance they could make no distinction between the innocent and the guilty.

On the 10th of October, 1717, a vessel containing a number of emigrants arrived at Philadelphia, a small but flourishing settlement upon the banks of the Delaware. Among the passengers there was a man named George Boone, with his wife and eleven children, nine sons and two daughters. He had come from Exeter, England, and was lured to the New World by the cheapness of land. He had sufficient property to enable him to furnish all his sons with ample farms in America. The Delaware, above Philadelphia, was at that time a silent stream, flowing sublimely through the almost unbroken forest. Here and there, a bold settler had felled the trees, and in the clearing had reared his log hut, upon the river banks. Occasionally the birch canoe of an Indian hunter was seen passing rapidly from cove to cove, and occasionally a little cluster of Indian wigwams graced some picturesque and sunny exposure, for the Indians manifested much taste in the location of their villages.

George Boone ascended this solitary river about twenty miles above Philadelphia, where he purchased upon its banks an extensive territory, consisting of several hundred acres. It was near the present city of Bristol, in what is now called Buck's County. To this tract, sufficiently large for a township, he gave the name of Exeter, in memory of the home he had left in England. Here, aided by the strong arms of his boys, he reared a commodious log cabin. It must have been an attractive and a happy home. The climate was delightful, the soil fertile, supplying him, with but little culture, with an ample supply of corn, and the most nutritious vegetables. Before his door rolled the broad expanse of the Delaware, abounding with fish of delicious flavor. His boys with hook and line could at any time, in a few moments, supply the table with a nice repast. With the unerring rifle, they could always procure game in great variety and abundance.

The Indians, won by the humanity of William Penn, were friendly, and their occasional visits to the cabin contributed to the enjoyment of its inmates. On the whole a more favored lot in life could not well be imagined. There was unquestionably far more happiness in this log cabin of the settler, on the silent waters of the Delaware, than could be found in any of the castles or palaces of England, France, or Spain.

George Boone had one son on whom he conferred the singular name of Squire. His son married a young woman in the neighborhood by the name of Sarah Morgan, and surrounded by his brothers and sisters, he raised his humble home in the beautiful township which his father had purchased. Before leaving England the family, religiously inclined, had accepted the Episcopal form of Christian worship. But in the New World, far removed from the institutions of the Gospel, and allured by the noble character and influence of William Penn, they enrolled themselves in the Society of Friends. In the record of the monthly meetings of this society, we find it stated that George Boone was received to its communion on the thirty-first day of tenth month, in the year 1717. It is also recorded that his son Squire Boone was married to Sarah Morgan, on the twenty-third day of seventh month, 1720. The records of the meetings also show the number of their children, and the periods of their birth.

By this it appears that their son Daniel, the subject of this memoir, was born on the twenty-second day of eighth month, 1734. It seems that Squire Boone became involved in difficulties with the Society of Friends, for allowing one of his sons to marry out of meeting. He was therefore disowned, and perhaps on this account, he subsequently removed his residence to North Carolina, as we shall hereafter show. His son Daniel, from earliest childhood, developed a peculiar and remarkably interesting character. He was silent, thoughtful, of pensive temperament, yet far from gloomy, never elated, never depressed. He exhibited from his earliest years such an insensibility to danger, as to attract the attention of all who knew him. Though affectionate and genial in disposition, never morose or moody, he still loved solitude, and seemed never so happy as when entirely alone. His father remained in his home upon the Delaware until Daniel was about ten years of age.

Various stories are related of his adventures in these his early years, which may or may not be entirely authentic. It makes but little difference. These anecdotes if only founded on facts, show at least the estimation in which he was regarded, and the impression which his character produced in these days of childhood. Before he was ten years old he would take his rifle and plunge boldly into the depths of the illimitable forest. He seemed, by instinct, possessed of the skill of the most experienced hunter, so that he never became bewildered, or in danger of being lost. There were panthers, bears and wolves in those forests, but of them he seemed not to have the slightest fear. His skill as a marksman became quite unerring. Not only raccoons, squirrels, partridges and other such small game were the result of his hunting expeditions, but occasionally even the fierce panther fell before his rifle ball. From such frequent expeditions he would return silent and tranquil, with never a word of boasting in view of exploits of which a veteran hunter might be proud.

Indeed his love of solitude was so great, that he reared for himself a little cabin in the wilderness, three miles back from the settlement. Here he would go all alone without even a dog for companion, his trusty rifle his only protection. At his camp-fire, on the point of his ramrod, he would cook the game which he obtained in abundance, and upon his bed of leaves would sleep in sweetest enjoyment, lulled by the wind through the tree-tops, and by the cry of the night bird and of the wild beasts roaming around. In subsequent life, he occasionally spoke of these hours as seasons of unspeakable joy.

The education of young Boone was necessarily very defective. There were no schools then established in those remote districts of log cabins. But it so happened that an Irishman of some little education strolled into that neighborhood, and Squire Boone engaged him to teach, for a few months, his children and those of some others of the adjacent settlers. These hardy emigrants met with their axes in a central point in the wilderness, and in a few hours constructed a rude hut of logs for a school-house. Here young Boone was taught to read, and perhaps to write. This was about all the education he ever received. Probably the confinement of the school-room was to him unendurable. The forest was his congenial home, hunting the business of his life.

Though thus uninstructed in the learning of books, there were other parts of practical education, of infinitely more importance to him, in which he became an adept. His native strength of mind, keen habits of observation, and imperturbable tranquility under whatever perils or reverses, gave him skill in the life upon which he was to enter, which the teachings of books alone could not confer. No marksman could surpass him in the dexterity with which with his bullet he would strike the head of a nail, at the distance of many yards. No Indian hunter or warrior could with more sagacity trace his steps through the pathless forest, detect the footsteps of a retreating foe, or search out the hiding place of the panther or the bear. In these hunting excursions the youthful frame of Daniel became inured to privation, hardship, endurance. Taught to rely upon his own resources, he knew not what it was to be lonely, for an hour. In the darkest night and in the remotest wilderness, when the storm raged most fiercely, although but a child he felt peaceful, happy, and entirely at home.

About the year 1748 (the date is somewhat uncertain), Squire Boone, with his family, emigrated seven hundred miles farther south and west to a place called Holman's Ford on the Yadkin river, in North Carolina. The Yadkin is a small stream in the north-west part of the State. A hundred years ago this was indeed a howling wilderness. It is difficult to imagine what could have induced the father of a family to abandon the comparatively safe and prosperous settlements on the banks of the Delaware, to plunge into the wilderness of these pathless solitudes, several hundred miles from the Atlantic coast. Daniel was then about sixteen years of age.

Of the incidents of their long journey through the wood—on foot, with possibly a few pack horses, for there were no wagon-roads whatever—we have no record. The journey must probably have occupied several weeks, occasionally cheered by sunshine, and again drenched by storms. There were nine children in the family. At the close of the weary pilgrimage of a day, through such narrow trails as that which the Indian or the buffalo had made through the forest, or over the prairies, they were compelled to build a cabin at night, with logs and the bark of trees to shelter them from the wind and rain, and at the camp-fire to cook the game which they had shot during the day. We can imagine that this journey must have been a season of unspeakable delight to Daniel Boone. Alike at home with the rifle and the hatchet, never for a moment bewildered, or losing his self-possession, he could, even unaided, at any hour, rear a sheltering hut for his mother and his sisters, before which the camp-fire would blaze cheerily, and their hunger would be appeased by the choicest viands from the game which his rifle had procured.

The spirit of adventure is so strong in most human hearts which luxurious indulgence has not enervated, that it is not improbable that this family enjoyed far more in this romantic excursion through an unexplored wilderness, than those now enjoy who in a few hours traverse the same distance in the smooth rolling rail-cars. Indeed fancy can paint many scenes of picturesque beauty which we know that the reality must have surpassed.

It is the close of a lovely day. A gentle breeze sweeps through the tree-tops from the north-west. The trail through the day has led along the banks of a crystal mountain stream, sparkling with trout. The path is smooth for the moccasined feet. The limbs, inured to action, experienced no weariness. The axes of the father and the sons speedily construct a camp, open to the south and perfectly sheltered on the roof and on the sides by the bark of trees. The busy fingers of the daughters have in the meantime spread over the floor a soft and fragrant carpet of evergreen twigs. The mother is preparing supper, of trout from the stream, and the fattest of wild turkeys or partridges, or tender cuts of venison, which the rifles of her husband or sons have procured. Voracious appetites render the repast far more palatable than the choicest viands which were ever spread in the banqueting halls of Versailles or Windsor. Water-fowl of gorgeous plumage sport in the stream, unintimidated by the approach of man. The plaintive songs of forest-birds float in the evening air. On the opposite side of the stream, herds of deer and buffalo crop the rich herbage of the prairie, which extends far away, till it is lost in the horizon of the south. Daniel retires from the converse of the cabin to an adjoining eminence, where silently and rapturously he gazes upon the scene of loveliness spread out before him.

Such incidents must often have occurred. Even in the dark and tempestuous night, with the storm surging through the tree tops, and the rain descending in floods, in their sheltered camp, illumined by the flames of their night fire, souls capable of appreciating the sublimity of such scenes must have experienced exquisite delight. It is pleasant to reflect, that the poor man in his humble cabin may often be the recipient of much more happiness than the lord finds in his castle, or the king in his palace.

No details are given respecting the arrival of this family on the banks of the Yadkin, or of their habits of life while there. We simply know that they were far away in the untrodden wilderness, in the remotest frontiers of civilization. Bands of Indians were roving around them, but even if hostile, so long as they had only bows and arrows, the settler in his log-hut, which was a fortress, and with his death-dealing rifle, was comparatively safe.

Here the family dwelt for several years, probably in the enjoyment of abundance, and with ever-increasing comforts. The virgin soil, even poorly tilled, furnished them with the corn and the vegetables they required, while the forests supplied the table with game. Thus the family, occupying the double position of the farmer and the hunter, lived in the enjoyment of all the luxuries which both of those callings could afford. Here Daniel Boone grew up to manhood. His love of solitude and of nature led him on long hunting excursions, from which he often returned laden with furs. The silence of the wilderness he brought back with him to his home. And though his placid features ever bore a smile, he had but few words to interchange with neighbors or friends. He was a man of affectionate, but not of passionate nature. It would seem that other emigrants were lured to the banks of the Yadkin, for here, after a few years, young Boone fell in love with the daughter of his father's neighbor, and that daughter, Rebecca Bryan, became his bride. He thus left his father's home, and, with his axe, speedily erected for himself and wife a cabin, we may presume at some distance from sight or sound of any other house. There "from noise and tumult far," Daniel Boone established himself in the life of solitude, to which he was accustomed and which he enjoyed. It appears that his marriage took place about the year 1755. The tide of emigration was still flowing in an uninterrupted stream towards the west. The population was increasing throughout this remote region, and the axe of the settler began to be heard on the streams tributary to the Yadkin.

Daniel Boone became restless. He loved the wilderness and its solitude, and was annoyed by the approach of human habitations, bringing to him customs with which he was unacquainted, and exposing him to embarrassments from which he would gladly escape. The mode of life practiced by those early settlers in the wilderness is well known. The log-house usually consisted of but one room, with a fire-place of stones at the end. These houses were often very warm and comfortable, presenting in the interior, with a bright fire blazing on the hearth, a very cheerful aspect. Their construction was usually as follows: Straight, smooth logs about a foot in diameter, cut of the proper length, and so notched at the ends as to be held very firmly together, were thus placed one above the other to the height of about ten feet. The interstices were filled with clay, which soon hardened, rendering the walls comparatively smooth, and alike impervious to wind or rain. Other logs of straight fiber were split into clap-boards, one or two inches in thickness, with which they covered the roof. If suitable wood for this purpose could not be found, the bark of trees was used, with an occasional thatching of the long grass of the prairies. Logs about eighteen inches in diameter were selected for the floor. These were easily split in halves, and with the convex side buried in the earth, and the smooth surface uppermost joined closely together by a slight trimming with axe or adze, presented a very firm and even attractive surface for the feet.

In the centre of the room, four augur holes were bored in the logs, about three inches in diameter. Stakes were driven firmly into these holes, upon which were placed two pieces of timber, with the upper surfaces hewn smooth, thus constructing a table. In one corner of the cabin, four stakes were driven in a similar way, about eighteen inches high, with forked tops. Upon these two saplings were laid with smooth pieces of bark stretched across. These were covered with grass or dried leaves, upon which was placed, with the fur upwards, the well-tanned skin of the buffalo or the bear. Thus quite a luxurious bed was constructed, upon which there was often enjoyed as sweet sleep as perhaps is ever found on beds of down. In another corner, some rude shelves were placed, upon which appeared a few articles of tin and ironware. Upon some buck horns over the door was always placed the rifle, ever loaded and ready for use.

A very intelligent emigrant, Dr. Doddridge, gives the following graphic account of his experience in such a log-cabin as we have described, in the remote wilderness. When he was but a child, his father, with a small family, had penetrated these trackless wilds, and in the midst of their sublime solitudes had reared his lonely cabin. He writes:

"My father's family was small and he took us all with him. The Indian meal which he brought was expended six weeks too soon, so that for that length of time we had to live without bread. The lean venison and the breast of wild turkeys, we were taught to call bread. I remember how narrowly we children watched the growth of the potato tops, pumpkin, and squash vines, hoping from day to day to get something to answer in the place of bread. How delicious was the taste of the young potatoes, when we got them! What a jubilee when we were permitted to pull the young corn for roasting ears! Still more so when it had acquired sufficient hardness to be made into johnny cake by the aid of a tin grater. The furniture of the table consisted of a few pewter dishes, plates and spoons, but mostly of wooden bowls and trenchers and noggins. If these last were scarce, gourds and hard shell squashes made up the deficiency.

"I well remember the first time I ever saw a tea cup and saucer. My mother died when I was six or seven years of age. My father then sent me to Maryland to go to school. At Bedford, the tavern at which my uncle put up was a stone house, and to make the changes still more complete, it was plastered on the inside both as to the walls and ceiling. On going into the dining-room, I was struck with astonishment at the appearance of the house. I had no idea that there was any house in the world that was not built of logs. But here I looked around and could see no logs, and above I could see no joists. Whether such a thing had been made by the hands of man, or had grown so of itself, I could not conjecture. I had not the courage to inquire anything about it. When supper came on, my confusion was worse confounded: A little cup stood in a bigger one with some brownish-looking stuff in it, which was neither milk, hominy, nor broth. What to do with these little cups, and the spoons belonging to them, I could not tell. But I was afraid to ask anything concerning the use of them."

Daniel Boone could see from the door of his cabin, far away in the west, the majestic ridge of the Alleghany Mountains, many of the peaks rising six thousand feet into the clouds. This almost impassable wall, which nature had reared, extended for hundreds of leagues, along the Atlantic coast, parallel with that coast, and at an average distance of one hundred and thirty miles from the ocean. It divides the waters which flow into the Atlantic, from those which run into the Mississippi. The great chain consists of many spurs, from fifty to two hundred miles in breadth, and receives in different localities, different names, such as the Cumberland Mountains, the Blue Ridge, etc.

But few white men had ever as yet ascended these summits, to cast a glance at the vast wilderness beyond. The wildest stories were told around the cabin fires, of these unexplored realms,—of the Indian tribes wandering there; of the forests filled with game; of the rivers alive with fishes; of the fertile plains, the floral beauty, the abounding fruit, and the almost celestial clime. These stories were brought to the settlers in the broken language of the Indians, and in the exaggerated tales of hunters, who professed that in the chase they had, from some Pisgah's summit, gazed upon the splendors of this Canaan of the New World.

Thus far, the settlers had rested contented with the sea-board region east of the Alleghanies. They had made no attempt to climb the summits of this great barrier, or to penetrate its gloomy defiles. A dense forest covered alike the mountain cliff and the rocky gorge. Indeed there were but few points at which even the foot of the hunter could pass this chain.

While Daniel Boone was residing in the congenial solitude of his hut, on the banks of the Yadkin; with the grandeur of the wilderness around him in which his soul delighted; with his table luxuriously spread according to his tastes—with venison, bear's meat, fat turkeys, chickens from the prairie, and vegetables from his garden; with comfortable clothing of deerskin, and such cloths as pedlars occasionally brought to his cabin door in exchange for furs, he was quite annoyed by the arrival of a number of Scotch families in his region, bringing with them customs and fashions which to Daniel Boone were very annoying. They began to cut down the glorious old forest, to break up the green sward of the prairies, to rear more ambitious houses than the humble home of the pioneer; they assumed airs of superiority, introduced more artificial styles of living, and brought in the hitherto unknown vexation of taxes.

One can easily imagine how restive such a man as Boone must have been under such innovations. The sheriff made his appearance in the lonely hut; the collection of the taxes was enforced by suits at law. Even Daniel Boone's title to his lands was called in question; some of the new comers claiming that their more legal grants lapped over upon the boundaries which Boone claimed. Under these circumstances our pioneer became very anxious to escape from these vexations by an emigration farther into the wilderness. Day after day he cast wistful glances upon the vast mountain barrier piercing the clouds in the distant horizon. Beyond that barrier, neither the sheriff nor the tax-gatherer were to be encountered. His soul, naturally incapable of fear, experienced no dread in apprehension of Indian hostilities, or the ferocity of wild beasts. Even the idea of the journey through these sublime solitudes of an unexplored region, was far more attractive to him than the tour of Europe to a sated millionaire.

Two or three horses would convey upon their backs all their household goods. There were Indian trails and streets, so called, made by the buffaloes, as in large numbers they had followed each other, selecting by a wonderful instinct their path from one feeding ground to another, through cane-brakes, around morasses, and over mountains through the most accessible defiles. Along these trails or streets, Boone could take his peaceful route without any danger of mistaking his way. Every mile would be opening to him new scenes of grandeur and beauty. Should night come, or a storm set in, a few hours' labor with his axe would rear for him not only a comfortable, but a cheerful tent with its warm and sheltered interior, with the camp-fire crackling and blazing before it. His wife and his children not only afforded him all the society his peculiar nature craved, but each one was a helper, knowing exactly what to do in this picnic excursion through the wilderness. Wherever he might stop for the night or for a few days, his unerring rifle procured for him viands which might tempt the appetite of the epicure. There are many even in civilized life who will confess, that for them, such an excursion would present attractions such as are not to be found in the banqueting halls at Windsor Castle, or in the gorgeous saloons of Versailles.

Daniel Boone, in imagination, was incessantly visiting the land beyond the mountains, and longing to explore its mysteries. Whether he would find the ocean there or an expanse of lakes and majestic rivers, or boundless prairies, or the unbroken forest, he knew not. Whether the region were crowded with Indians, and if so, whether they would be found friendly or hostile, and whether game roamed there in greater variety and in larger abundance than on the Atlantic side of the great barrier, were questions as yet all unsolved. But these questions Daniel Boone pondered in silence, night and day.

A gentleman who nearly half a century ago visited one of these frontier dwellings, very romantically situated amidst the mountains of Western Virginia, has given us a pencil sketch of the habitation which we here introduce. The account of the visit is also so graphic that we cannot improve it by giving it in any language but his own. This settler had passed through the first and was entering upon the second stage of pioneer life:

> "Towards the close of an autumnal day, when traveling through the thinly settled region of Western Virginia, I came up with a substantial-looking farmer leaning on the fence by the road side. I accompanied him to his house to spend the night. It was a log dwelling, and near it stood another log structure, about twelve feet square,—the weaving shop of the family. On entering the dwelling I found the numerous household all clothed in substantial garments of their own manufacture. The floor was unadorned by a carpet and the room devoid of superfluous furniture; yet they had all that necessity required for their comfort. One needs but little experience like this to learn how few are our real wants,—how easily most luxuries of dress, furniture and equipage can be dispensed with.
>
> "Soon after my arrival supper was ready. It consisted of fowls, bacon, hoe-cake and buckwheat cakes. Our beverage was milk and

coffee, sweetened with maple sugar. Soon as it grew dark my hostess took down a small candle mould for three candles, hanging from the wall on a frame-work just in front of the fire-place, in company with a rifle, long strings of dried pumpkins and other articles of household property. On retiring I was conducted to the room overhead, to which I ascended by stairs out of doors. My bed-fellow was the county sheriff, a young man of about my own age. And as we lay together a fine field was had for astronomical observations through the chinks of the logs.

"The next morning, after rising, I was looking for the washing apparatus, when he tapped me on the shoulder, as a signal to accompany him to the brook in the rear of the house, in whose pure crystal waters we performed our morning ablutions. After breakfast, through the persuasion of the sheriff, I agreed to go across the country by his house. He was on horseback; I on foot bearing my knapsack. For six miles our route lay through a pathless forest; on emerging from which we soon passed through the 'Court House,' the only village in the county, consisting of about a dozen log-houses and the court building.

"Soon after we came to a Methodist encampment. This was formed of three continuous lines, each occupying a side of a square and about one hundred feet in length. Each row was divided into six or ten cabins with partitions between. The height of the rows on the inner side of the enclosed area was about ten feet, on the outer about six, to which the roofs sloped shed-like. The door of each cabin opened on the inner side of the area, and at the back of each was a log chimney coming up even with the roof. At the upper extremity of the inclosure, formed by these three lines of cabins, was an open shed; a mere roof supported by posts, say thirty by fifty feet, in which was a coarse pulpit and log seats. A few tall trees were standing within the area, and many stumps scattered here and there. The whole establishment was in the depth of a forest, and wild and rude as can well be imagined.

"In many of these sparsely-inhabited counties there are no settled clergy, and rarely do the people hear any other than the Methodist preachers. Here is the itinerating system of Wesley exhibited in its full usefulness. The circuits are usually of three weeks' duration, in which the clergymen preach daily. Most of these preachers are energetic, devoted men; and often they endure great privations.

"After sketching the encampment I came in a few moments to the dwelling of the sheriff. Close by it was a group of mountain men and women seated around a log cabin, about twelve feet square, ten high, and open at the top, into which these neighbors of my companion were casting ears of corn as fast as they could shuck them. Cheerfully they performed their task. The men were large and hardy; the damsels plump and rosy, and all dressed in good warm homespun. The sheriff informed me that he owned about two thousand acres around his dwelling, and that his farm was worth about one thousand dollars or fifty cents an acre.

"I entered his log domicile which was one story in height, about twenty feet square and divided into two small rooms without windows or places to let in the light except by a front and rear door. I soon partook of a meal in which we had a variety of luxuries, not omitting *bear's meat*. A blessing was asked at the table by one of the neighbors. After supper the bottle, as usual at corn huskings, was circulated. The sheriff learning that I was a Washingtonian, with the politeness of one of nature's gentlemen refrained from urging me to participate. The men drank but moderately; and we all drew around the fire, the light of which was the only one we had. Hunting stories and kindred topics served to talk down the hours till bed time.

"On awaking in the morning, I saw two women cooking breakfast in my bedroom, and three men seated over the fire watching the operation. After breakfast, I bade my host farewell, buckled on my knapsack and left. In the course of two hours, I came to a cabin by the wayside. There being no gate, I sprang over the fence, entered the open door, and was received with a hearty welcome. It was an humble dwelling, the abode of poverty. The few articles of furniture were neat and pleasantly arranged. In the corner stood two beds, one hung with curtains, and both with coverlets of snowy white, contrasting with the dingy log walls, rude furniture, and rough boarded floor of this, the only room in the dwelling. Around a cheerful fire was seated an interesting family group. In one corner, on the hearth, sat the mother, smoking a pipe. Next to her was a little girl, in a small chair, holding a young kitten. In the opposite corner sat a venerable old man, of herculean stature, robed in a hunting shirt, and with a countenance as majestic and impressive as that of a Roman senator. In the centre of the group was a young maiden, modest and retiring, not beautiful, except in that moral beauty virtue gives. She was reading to them from a little book. She was the only one of the family who could read, and she could do so but imperfectly. In that small volume was the whole secret of the neatness and happiness found in this lonely cot. That little book was the New Testament."

The institution of camp-meetings, introduced with so much success by the Methodists, those noble pioneers of Christianity, seem to have been the necessary result of the attempt to preach to the sparsely settled population of a new country. The following is said to be the origin of those camp-meetings which have done incalculable good, socially, intellectually, and religiously.

In the year 1799, two men by the name of McGee, one a Presbyterian, the other a Methodist, set out on a missionary tour together, to visit the log-houses in the wilderness. A meeting was appointed at a little settlement upon one of the tributaries of the Ohio. The pioneers flocked to the place from many miles around. There was no church there, and the meeting was necessarily held in the open air. Many brought their food with them and camped out. Thus the meeting, with exhortation and prayer, was continued in the night. Immense bonfires blazed illuminating the sublimities of the forest, and the assembled congregation, cut off from all the ordinary privileges of civilized life, listened devoutly to the story of a Savior's love.

This meeting was so successful in its results that another was appointed at a small settlement on the banks of a stream called Muddy River. The tidings spread rapidly through all the stations and farm houses on the frontier. It afforded these lonely settlers a delightful opportunity of meeting together. They could listen for hours with unabated interest to the religious exercises. The people assembled from a distance of forty or fifty miles around. A vast concourse had met beneath the foliage of the trees, the skies alone, draped with clouds by day and adorned with stars by night, the dome of their majestic temple.

The scene, by night, must have been picturesque in the extreme. Men, women and children were there in homespun garb; and being accustomed to camp life, they were there in comfort. Strangers met and became friends. Many wives and mothers obtained rest and refreshment from their monotonous toils. There is a bond in Christ's discipleship, stronger than any other, and Christians grasped hands in love, pledging themselves anew to a holy life. For several days and nights, this religious festival was continued. Time could not have been better spent. Dwellers in the forest could not afford to take so long a journey merely to listen to one half-hour's discourse. These men and women were earnest and thoughtful. In the solitude of their homes, they had reflected deeply upon life and its issues. When death occasionally visited their cabins, it was a far more awful event than when death occurs in the crowded city, where the hearse is every hour of every day passing through the streets.

These scenes of worship very deeply impressed the minds of the people. They were not Gospel hardened. The gloom and silence of the forest, alike still by night and by day; the memory of the past, with its few joys and many griefs; the anticipations of the future, with its unceasing struggles, to terminate only in death; the solemnity which rested on every countenance; the sweet melody of the hymns; the earnest tones of the preachers in exhortation and prayer, all combined to present a scene calculated to produce a very profound impression upon the human mind. At this meeting, not only professed Christians were greatly revived, but not less than a hundred persons, it was thought, became disciples of the Savior.

Another camp-meeting was soon after appointed to meet on Desha's Creek, a small stream flowing into the Cumberland River. The country was now becoming more populous, and several thousand were assembled. And thus the work went on, multitudes being thus reached by the preached Gospel who could not be reached in any other way.[1]

Life on the frontier was by no means devoid of its enjoyments as well as of its intense excitements. It must have been also an exceedingly busy life. There were no mills for cutting timber or grinding corn; no blacksmith shops to repair the farming utensils. There were no tanneries, no carpenters, shoemakers, weavers. Every family had to do everything for itself. The corn was pounded with a heavy pestle in a large mortar made by burning an excavation in a solid block of wood. By means of these mortars

---

[1] Bang's *History of Methodism.*

the settlers, in regions where saltpetre could be obtained, made very respectable gunpowder. In making corn-meal a grater was sometimes used, consisting of a half-circular piece of tin, perforated with a punch from the concave side. The ears of corn were rubbed on the rough edges, and the meal fell through the holes on a board or cloth placed to receive it. They also sometimes made use of a handmill, resembling those alluded to in the Bible. These consisted of two circular stones; the lowest, which was immovable, was called the bed-stone,—the upper one, the runner. Two persons could grind together at this mill.

The clothing was all of domestic manufacture. A fabric called linsey-woolsey was most frequently in use and made the most substantial and warmest clothing. It was made of flax and wool, the former the warp, the latter the filling. Every cabin almost had its rude loom, and every woman was a weaver.

The men tanned their own leather. A large trough was sunk in the ground to its upper edge. Bark was shaved with an axe and pounded with a mallet. Ashes were used for lime in removing the hair. In the winter evenings the men made strong shoes and moccasins, and the women cut out and made hunting shirts, leggins and drawers.

Hunting was a great source of amusement as well as a very exciting and profitable employment. The boys were all taught to imitate the call of every bird and beast in the woods. The skill in imitation which they thus acquired was wonderful. Hidden in a thicket they would gobble like a turkey and lure a whole flock of these birds within reach of their rifles. Bleating like the fawn they would draw the timid dam to her death. The moping owls would come in flocks attracted by the screech of the hunter, while packs of wolves, far away in the forest, would howl in response to the hunter's cry. The boys also rivalled the Indians in the skill with which they would throw the tomahawk. With a handle of a given length, and measuring the distance with the eye, they would throw the weapon with such accuracy that its keen edge would be sure to strike the object at which it was aimed. Running, jumping, wrestling were pastimes in which both boys and men engaged. Shooting at a mark was one of the most favorite diversions. When a boy had attained the age of about twelve years, a rifle was usually placed in his hands. In the house or fort where he resided, a port-hole was assigned him, where he was to do valiant service as a soldier, in case of an attack by the Indians. Every day he was in the woods hunting squirrels, turkeys and raccoons. Thus he soon acquired extraordinary expertness with his gun.

The following interesting narrative is taken from Ramsay's Annals of Tennessee, which State was settled about the same time with Kentucky and with emigrants from about the same region:

> "The settlement of Tennessee was unlike that of the present new country of the United States. Emigrants from the Atlantic cities, and from most points in the Western interior, now embark upon steamboats or other craft, and carrying with them all the conveniences and comforts of civilized life—indeed many of its luxuries—are, in a few days, without toil, danger or exposure, transported to their new abodes, and in a few months are surrounded with the appendages of home, of civilization and the blessings of law and of society.
>
> "The wilds of Minnesota and Nebraska, by the agency of steam or the stalwart arms of Western boatmen, are at once transformed into the settlements of a commercial and civilized people. Independence and Saint Paul, six months after they are laid off, have their stores and their workshops, their artisans and their mechanics. The mantua-maker and the tailor arrive in the same boat with the carpenter and mason. The professional man and the printer quickly follow. In the succeeding year the piano, the drawing-room, the restaurant, the billiard table, the church bell, the village and the city in miniature are all found, while the neighboring interior is yet a wilderness and a desert.
>
> "The town and comfort, taste and urbanity are first; the clearing, the farm house, the wagon road and the improved country, second. It was far different on the frontier of Tennessee. At first a single Indian trail was the only entrance to the Eastern border of it, and for many years admitted only the hunter and the pack-horse. It was not till the year 1776 that a wagon was seen in Tennessee. In consequence of the want of roads—as well as of the great distance from the sources of supply—the first inhabitants were without tools, and of course without mechanics—much more without the conveniences of living and the comforts of housekeeping.

"Luxuries were absolutely unknown. Salt was brought on packhorses from Augusta and Richmond and readily commanded ten dollars a bushel. The salt gourd in every cabin was considered as a treasure. The sugar maple furnished the only article of luxury on the frontier; coffee and tea being unknown or beyond the reach of the settlers. Sugar was seldom made and was used only for the sick, or in the preparation of a sweetened dram at a wedding, or on the arrival of a new comer.

"The appendages of the kitchen, the cupboard and the table, were scanty and simple. Iron was brought at great expense from the forges east of the mountains, on pack-horses, and was sold at an enormous price. Its use was, for this reason, confined to the construction and repair of ploughs and other farming utensils. Hinges, nails and fastenings of that material were seldom seen. The costume of the first settlers corresponded well with the style of their buildings and the quality of their furniture: the hunting shirt of the militia man and the hunter was in general use. The rest of their apparel was in keeping with it,—plain, substantial and well adapted for comfort, use and economy. The apparel of the pioneer's family was all home-made; and in a whole neighborhood there would not be seen, at the first settlement of the country, a single article of dress of foreign manufacture. Half the year, in many families, shoes were not worn. Boots, a fur hat and a coat, with buttons on each side, attracted the gaze of the beholder and sometimes received censure or rebuke. A stranger from the old States chose to doff his ruffles, his broad-cloth and his cue rather than endure the scoff and ridicule of the backwoodsman.

"The dwelling house on every frontier in Tennessee was the log-cabin. A carpenter and a mason were not needed to build them—much less the painter, the glazier and the upholsterer. Every settler had, besides his rifle, no other instrument but an axe or hatchet and a butcher-knife. A saw, an auger, a file and a broad-axe would supply a whole settlement, and were used as common property in the erection of the log-cabin.

"The labor and employment of a pioneer family were distributed in accordance with surrounding circumstances. To the men was assigned the duty of procuring subsistence and materials for clothing, erecting the cabin and the station, opening and cultivating the farm, hunting the wild beasts, and repelling and pursueing the Indians. The women spun the flax, the cotton and the wool, wove the cloth, made them up, milked, churned and prepared the food, and did their full share of the duties of housekeeping.

"Could there be happiness or comfort in such dwellings and such a state of society? To those who are accustomed to modern refinements the truth appears like fable. The early occupants of log-cabins were among the most happy of mankind. Exercise and excitement gave them health. They were practically equal, common danger made them mutually dependent. Brilliant hopes of future wealth and distinction led them on. And as there was ample room for all, and as each new comer increased individual and general security, there was little room for that envy, jealousy and hatred which constitute a large portion of human misery in older societies.

"Never were the story, the joke, the song and the laugh better enjoyed than upon the hewed blocks or puncheon stools, around the roaring log fire of the early western settler.

"On the frontier the diet was necessarily plain and homely, but exceedingly abundant and nutritive. The Goshen of America furnishes the richest milk and the most savory and delicious meats. In their rude cabins, with their scanty and inartificial furniture, no people ever enjoyed, in wholesome food a greater variety, or a superior quality of the necessaries of life."

A writer of that day describes the sports of these pioneers of Kentucky. One of them consisted in "driving the nail." A common nail was hammered into a target for about two thirds of its length. The marksmen then took their stand at the distance of about forty paces. Each man carefully cleaned the interior of his gun, and then placed a bullet in his hand, over which he poured just enough powder to cover it. This was a charge. A shot which only came close to the nail was considered a very indifferent shot. Nothing was deemed satisfactory but striking the nail with the bullet fairly on the head. Generally one out of three shots would hit the nail. Two nails were frequently needed before each man could get a shot.

Barking of Squirrels is another sport. "I first witnessed," writes the one to whom we have above alluded, "this manner of procuring squirrels, while near the town of Frankfort. The performer was the celebrated Daniel Boone. We walked out together and followed the rocky margins of the

Kentucky River, until we reached a piece of flat land, thickly covered with black walnuts, oaks, and hickories. Squirrels were seen gambolling on every tree around us. My companion Mr. Boone, a stout, hale, athletic man, dressed in a homespun hunting shirt, bare legged and moccasined, carried a long and heavy rifle, which, as he was loading it, he said had proved efficient in all his former undertakings, and which he hoped would not fail on this occasion, as he felt proud to show me his skill.

"The gun was wiped, the powder measured, the ball patched with six hundred thread linen, and a charge sent home with a hickory rod. We moved not a step from the place, for the squirrels were so thick, that it was unnecessary to go after them. Boone pointed to one of these animals, which had observed us and was crouched on a tree, about fifty paces distant, and bade me mark well where the ball should hit. He raised his piece gradually, until the head, or sight of the barrel, was brought to a line with the spot he intended to strike. The whip-like report resounded through the woods, and along the hills, in repeated echoes. Judge of my surprise, when I perceived that the ball had hit the piece of bark immediately underneath the squirrel, and shivered it into splinters; the concussion produced by which had killed the animal, and sent it whirling through the air, as if it had been blown up by the explosion of a powder magazine, Boone kept up his firing, and before many hours had elapsed, we had procured as many squirrels as we wished. Since that first interview with the veteran Boone, I have seen many other individuals perform the same feat.

"The *Snuffing of a Candle* with a ball, I first had an opportunity of seeing near the banks of Green River, not far from a large pigeon roost, to which I had previously made a visit. I had heard many reports of guns during the early part of a dark night, and knowing them to be rifles, I went towards the spot to ascertain the cause. On reaching the place, I was welcomed by a dozen tall, stout men, who told me they were exercising for the purpose of enabling them to shoot in the night at the reflected light from the eyes of a deer, or wolf, by torch-light.

"A fire was blazing near, the smoke of which rose curling among the thick foliage of the trees. At a distance which rendered it scarcely distinguishable, stood a burning candle, which in reality was only fifty yards from the spot on which we all stood. One man was within a few yards of it to watch the effect of the shots, as well as to light the candle, should it chance to go out, or to replace it should the shot cut it across. Each marksman shot in his turn. Some never hit neither the snuff or the candle, and were congratulated with a loud laugh; while others actually snuffed the candle without putting it out, and were recompensed for their dexterity with numerous hurrahs. One of them, who was particularly expert, was very fortunate and snuffed the candle three times out of seven; while all the other shots either put out the candle or cut it immediately under the light."

Chapter 3

LOUISIANA, ITS DISCOVERY AND VICISSITUDES

The transfer of Louisiana to the United States is one of the most interesting events in the history of our country. In the year 1800, Spain, then in possession of the vast region west of the Mississippi, ceded it to France. The whole country west of the majestic river appropriately called the Father of Waters, was then called Louisiana, and its boundaries were very obscurely defined. Indeed neither the missionary nor the hunter had penetrated but a very short distance into those unknown wilds. It was in the year 1541 that De Soto, marching from Florida across the country, came to the banks of this magnificent river, near the present site of Memphis. He knew not where it took its rise, or where it emptied its swollen flood. But he found a stream more than a mile in width, of almost fathomless depth, rolling its rapid, turbid stream, on which were floated innumerable logs and trees, through an almost uninhabited country of wonderful luxuriance. He was in search of gold, and crossing the river, advanced in a northwesterly direction about two hundred miles, till he came within sight of the Highlands of the White River. He then turned in a southerly direction, and continued his explorations, till death soon terminated his melancholy career.

More than one hundred and thirty years passed over these solitudes, when James Marquette, a French missionary among the Indians at Saint Marys, the outlet of Lake Superior, resolved to explore the Mississippi, of whose magnificence he had heard much from the lips of the Indians, who had occasionally extended their hunting tours to its banks. He was inured to all the hardships of the wilderness, seemed to despise worldly comforts, and had a soul of bravery which could apparently set all perils at defiance. And still he was indued with a poetic nature, which reveled in the charms of these wild and romantic realms, as he climbed its mountains and floated in his canoe over its silent and placid streams. Even then it was not known whether the Mississippi emptied its majestic flood into the Pacific Ocean or into the Gulf of Mexico. The foot of the white man upon the shores of Lake Superior, had never penetrated beyond the Indian village, where the Fox River enters into Green Bay. From this point Marquette started for the exploration of the Mississippi. The party consisted of Mr. Marquette, a French gentleman by the name of Joliete, five French voyageurs and two Indian guides. They transported their two birch canoes on their shoulders across the portage from the Fox River to the Wisconsin River. Paddling rapidly down this stream through realms of silence and solitude, they soon entered the majestic Mississippi, more than fifteen hundred miles above its mouth.

Marquette seems to have experienced in the highest degree the romance of his wonderful voyage, for he says that he commenced the descent of the mighty river with "a joy that could not be expressed." It was the beautiful month of June, 1673, the most genial season of the year. The skies were bright above them. The placid stream was fringed with banks of wonderful luxuriance and beauty, the rocky cliffs at times assuming the aspect of majestic castles of every variety of architecture; again the gently swelling hills were robed in sublime forests, and again the smooth meadows, in their verdure, spread far away to the horizon. Rapidly the canoes, gently guided by the paddles, floated down the stream.

Having descended the river about one hundred and eighty miles, they came to a very well-trod Indian trail leading back from the river into the interior. Marquette and Joliete had the curiosity and the courage to follow this trail for six miles, until they came to an Indian village. It would seem that some of the Indians there, in their hunting excursions, had wandered to some of the French settlements; for four of their leading men, dressed in the most gorgeous display of barbaric pomp, "brilliant with many colored plumes," came out to meet them and conducted them to the cabin of their chief. He addressed them in the following words:

> "How beautiful is the sun, Frenchman, when thou comest to visit us. Our whole village welcomes thee. In peace thou shalt enter all our dwellings."

After a very pleasant visit they returned to their boats and resumed their voyage. They floated by the mouth of the turbid Missouri, little dreaming of the grandeur of the realms watered by that imperial stream and its tributaries. They passed the mouth of the Ohio, which they recognized as the *Belle Rivière*, which the Indians then called the Wabash. As they floated rapidly away towards the south they visited many Indian villages on the banks of the stream, where the devoted missionary, Marquette, endeavored to proclaim the gospel of Christ.

"I did not," says Marquette, "fear death. I should have esteemed it the greatest happiness to have died for the glory of God."

Thus they continued their exploration as far south as the mouth of the Arkansas River, where they were hospitably received in a very flourishing Indian village. Being now satisfied that the Mississippi river entered the Gulf of Mexico, somewhere between Florida and California, they returned to Green Bay by the route of the Illinois River. By taking advantage of the eddies, on either side of the stream, it was not difficult for them, in their light canoes, to make the ascent.

Marquette landed on the western banks of Lake Michigan to preach the gospel to a tribe of Indians called the Miames, residing near the present site of Chicago. Joliete returned to Quebec to announce the result of their discoveries. He was received with great rejoicing. The whole population flocked to the cathedral, where the *Te Deum* was sung.

Five years passed away, during which the great river flowed almost unthought of, through its vast and sombre wilderness. At length in the year 1678, La Salle received a commission from Louis the XIV of France to explore the Mississippi to its mouth. Having received from the king the command of Fort Frontenac, at the northern extremity of Lake Ontario, and a monopoly of the fur trade in all the countries he should discover, he sailed from Larochelle in a ship well-armed and abundantly supplied, in June, 1678. Ascending the St. Lawrence to Quebec, he repaired to Fort Frontenac. With a large number of men he paddled, in birch canoes, to the southern extremity of Lake Ontario, and, by a portage around the falls of Niagara, entered Lake Erie. Here he built a substantial vessel, called the *Griffin*, which was the first vessel ever launched upon the waters of that lake. Embarking in this vessel with forty men, in the month of September, a genial and gorgeous month in those latitudes, he traversed with favoring breezes the whole length of the lake, a voyage of two hundred and sixty-five miles, ascended the straits and passed through the Lake of St. Clair, and ran along the coast of Lake Huron three hundred and sixty miles to Michilimackinac, where the three majestic lakes, Superior, Michigan and Huron, form a junction.

Here a trading post was established, which subsequently attained world-wide renown, and to which the Indians flocked with their furs from almost boundless realms. Mr. Schoolcraft, who some years after visited this romantic spot, gives the following interesting account of the scenery and strange life witnessed there. As these phases of human life have now passed away, never to be renewed, it seems important that the memory of them should be perpetuated:

> "Nothing can present a more picturesque and refreshing spectacle to the traveler, wearied with the lifeless monotony of a voyage through Lake Huron, than the first sight of the island of Michilimackinac, which rises from the watery horizon in lofty bluffs imprinting a rugged outline along the sky and capped with a fortress on which the American flag is seen waving against the blue heavens. The name is a compound of the word *Misril*, signifying great, and *Mackinac* the Indian word for turtle, from a fancied resemblance of the island to a *great turtle* lying upon the water.

"It is a spot of much interest, aside from its romantic beauty, in consequence of its historical associations and natural curiosities. It is nine miles in circumference, and its extreme elevation above the lake is over three hundred feet. The town is pleasantly situated around a small bay at the southern extremity of the island, and contains a few hundred souls, which are sometimes swelled to one or two thousand by the influx of voyageurs, traders and Indians. On these occasions its beautiful harbor is seen checkered with American vessels at anchor, and Indian canoes rapidly shooting across the water in every direction.

"It was formerly the seat of an extensive fur trade; at present it is noted for the great amount of trout and white fish annually exported. Fort Mackinac stood on a rocky bluff overlooking the town. The ruins of Fort Holmes are on the apex of the island. It was built by the British in the war of 1812, under the name of Fort George, and was changed to its present appellation after the surrender to the Americans, in compliment to the memory of Major Holmes, who fell in the attack upon the island.

"The old town of Michilimackinac stood at the extreme point of the peninsula of Michigan, nine miles south of the island. Eight years before La Salle's expedition, Father Marquette, the French missionary, visited this spot with a party of Hurons, upon whom he prevailed to locate themselves. A fort was soon constructed, and became an important post. It continued to be the seat of the fur trade, and the undisturbed rendezvous of the Indian tribes during the whole period that the French exercised dominion over the Canadas."

Here at Michilimackinac, La Salle purchased a rich cargo of furs, exchanging for them his goods at an immense profit. The *Griffin*, laden with wealth, set out on her return and was wrecked by the way with total loss. La Salle with his companions had embarked in birch canoes, and descending Lake Michigan to near its southern extremity, they landed and erected a fort which they called Miamis. They then carried their canoes across to the Illinois River and paddled down that stream until they came near to the present site of Peoria, where they established another fort, which La Salle, grief-stricken in view of his loss, named *Crève-Cœur*, or Heartsore. Here the energetic and courageous adventurer left his men in winter quarters, while, with but three companions, he traversed the wilderness on foot, amidst the snows of winter, to Fort Frontenac, a distance of fifteen hundred miles. After an absence of several weeks, he returned with additional men and the means of building a large and substantial flat-bottomed boat, with which to descend the Illinois River to the Mississippi, and the latter stream to its mouth.

The romantic achievement was successfully accomplished. The banners of France were unfurled along the banks of the majestic river and upon the shores of the Gulf of Mexico. This whole region which France claimed by the right of discovery, was named in honor of the king of France, Louisiana. Its limits were necessarily quite undefined. In 1684, a French colony of two hundred and eighty persons was sent out to effect a settlement on the Lower Mississippi. Passing by the mouth of the river without discovering it, they landed in Texas, and took possession of the country in the name of the king of France. Disaster followed disaster. La Salle died, and the colonists were exterminated by the Indians. Not long after this, all the country west of the Mississippi was ceded by France to Spain, and again, some years after, was surrendered back again by Spain to France. We have not space here to allude to the details of these varied transactions. But this comprehensive record seems to be essential to the full understanding of the narrative upon which we have entered.

It was in the year 1763 that Louisiana was ceded, by France, to Spain. In the year 1800, it was yielded back to France, under Napoleon, by a secret article in the treaty of Sn. Ildefonso. It had now become a matter of infinite moment to the United States that the great Republic should have undisputed command of the Mississippi, from its source to its mouth. President Jefferson instructed our Minister at Paris, Robert Livingston, to negotiate with the French Government for the purchase of Louisiana. France was then at war with England. The British fleet swept triumphantly all the seas. Napoleon, conscious that he could not protect Louisiana from British arms, consented to the sale. We are informed that on the 10th of April, 1803, he summoned two of his ministers in council, and said to them:

"I am fully sensible of the value of Louisiana; and it was my wish to repair the error of the French diplomatists who abandoned it in 1763. I have scarcely recovered it before I run the risk of losing it. But if I am obliged to give it up it shall cost more to those who force me to part with it, than to those to whom I yield it. The English have despoiled France of all her Northern possessions in America, and now they covet those of the South. I am determined that they shall not have the Mississippi. Although Louisiana is but a trifle compared with their vast possessions in other parts of the globe, yet, judging from the vexation they have manifested on seeing it return to the power of France, I am certain that their first object will be to obtain possession of it.

"They will probably commence the war in that quarter. They have twenty vessels in the Gulf of Mexico, and our affairs in St. Domingo are daily getting worse, since the death of Le Clere. The conquest of Louisiana might be easily made, and I have not a moment to lose in putting it out of their reach. I am not sure but that they have already began an attack upon it. Such a measure would be in accordance with their habits; and in their place I should not wait. I am inclined, in order to deprive them of all prospect of ever possessing it, to cede it to the United States. Indeed I can hardly say I cede it, for I do not yet possess it. And if I wait but a short time, my enemies may leave me nothing but an empty title to grant to the Republic I wish to conciliate. They only ask for one city of Louisiana; but I consider the whole colony as lost. And I believe that in the hands of this rising power, it will be more useful to the political and even the commercial interests of France, than if I should attempt to retain it. Let me have both of your opinions upon this subject."

One of the ministers, Barbé Marbois, cordially approved of the plan of "cession." The other opposed it. After long deliberation, the conference was closed, without Napoleon making known his decision. The next day he sent for Barbé Marbois, and said to him:

"The season for deliberation is over. I have determined to part with Louisiana. I shall give up not only New Orleans, but the whole colony without reservation. That I do not undervalue Louisiana I have sufficiently proved, as the object of my first treaty with Spain was to recover it. But though I regret parting with it, I am convinced that it would be folly to persist in trying to keep it. I commission you, therefore, to negotiate this affair with the envoys of the United States. Do not wait the arrival of Mr. Munroe, but go this very day and confer with Mr. Livingston.

"Remember, however, that I need ample funds for carrying on the war; and I do not wish to commence it by levying new taxes. During the last century, France and Spain have incurred great expense in the improvement of Louisiana, for which her trade has never indemnified them. Large sums have been advanced to different companies, which have never returned to the treasury. It is fair that I should require payment for these. Were I to regulate my demands by the importance of this territory to the United States, they would be unbounded. But being obliged to part with it, I shall be moderate in my terms. Still, remember I must have fifty millions of francs ($10,000,000), and I will not consent to take less. I would rather make some desperate effort to preserve this fine country."

Negotiations commenced that day. Soon Mr. Munroe arrived. On the 30th of April, 1803, the treaty was signed, the United States paying fifteen million dollars for the entire territory. It was stipulated by Napoleon that Louisiana should be, as soon as possible, incorporated into the Union; and that its inhabitants should enjoy the same rights, privileges, and immunities as other citizens of the United States. The third article of the treaty, securing to them these benefits, was drawn up by Napoleon himself. He presented it to the plenipotentiaries with these words:

"Make it known to the people of Louisiana, that we regret to part with them; that we have stipulated for all the advantages they could desire; and that France, in giving them up, has insured to them the greatest of all. They could never have prospered under any European government, as they will when they become independent. But while they enjoy the privileges of liberty, let them ever remember that they are French, and preserve for their mother country that affection, which a common origin inspires."

This purchase was an immense acquisition to the United States. "I consider," said Mr. Livingston, "that from this day, the United States take rank with the first powers of Europe, and now she has entirely escaped from the power of England."

Napoleon was also well pleased with the transaction, "By this cession," he said, "I have secured the power of the United States, and given to England a maritime rival, who, at some future time, will humble her pride."

The boundaries of this unexampled purchase could not be clearly defined. There was not any known landmarks to which reference could be made. The United States thus had the sole claim to the vast territory west of the Mississippi, extending on the north through Oregon to the Pacific Ocean, and on the south to the Mexican dominions. From the day of the transfer, the natural resources of the great valley of the Mississippi began to be rapidly developed.

The accompanying map will enable the reader more fully to understand the geography of the above narrative.

Chapter 4

CAMP LIFE BEYOND THE ALLEGHANIES

In the year 1767, a bold hunter by the name of John Finley with two or three companions crossed the mountain range of the Alleghanies into the region beyond, now known as Kentucky. The mountains where he crossed, consisting of a series of parallel ridges, some of which were quite impassable save at particular points, presented a rugged expanse nearly fifty miles in breadth. It took many weary days for these moccassined feet to traverse the wild solitudes. The Indian avoids the mountains. He chooses the smooth prairie where the buffalo and the elk graze, and where the wild turkey, the grouse and the prairie chicken, wing their flight, or the banks of some placid stream over which he can glide in his birch canoe, and where fish of every variety can be taken. Indeed the Indians, with an eye for picturesque beauty, seldom reared their villages in the forest, whose glooms repelled them. Generally where the forest approached the stream, they clustered their wigwams in its edge, with the tranquil river and the open country spread out before them.

John Finley and his companions traversed the broad expanse of the Alleghanies, without meeting any signs of human life. The extreme western ridge of these parallel eminences or spurs, has received the name of the Cumberland Mountains. Passing through a gorge, which has since then become renowned in peace and war as Cumberland Gap, they entered upon a vast undulating expanse, of wonderful fertility and beauty. In its rivers, its plains, its forests, its gentle eminences, its bright skies and salubrious clime, it presented then, as now, as attractive a residence for man as this globe can furnish. Finley and his companions spent several months roving through this, to them, new Eden. Game of every variety abounded. Through some inexplicable reason, no Indians held possession of the country. But wandering tribes, whose homes and acknowledged territory were far away in the north, the west, and the south, were ever traversing these regions in hunting bands. They often met in bloody encounters. These conflicts were so frequent and so sanguinary, that this realm so highly favored of God for the promotion of all happiness, subsequently received the appropriate name of "The dark and bloody ground."

After an absence of many months, Finley and his companions returned to North Carolina, with the most glowing accounts of the new country which they had found. Their story of the beauty of those realms was so extravagant, that many regarded them as gross exaggerations. It subsequently appeared, however, that they were essentially true. A more lovely and attractive region cannot be found on earth. It is man's inhumanity to man, mainly, which has ever caused such countless millions to mourn.

Daniel Boone listened eagerly to the recital of John Finley and his associates. The story they told added fuel to the flame of emigration, which was already consuming him. He talked more and more earnestly of his desire to cross the mountains. We know not what were the emotions with which his wife was agitated, in view of her husband's increasing desire for another plunge into the wilderness. We simply know that through her whole career, she manifested the most tender solicitude to accommodate herself to the wishes of her beloved husband. Indeed he was a man peculiarly calculated to win a noble woman's love. Gentle in his demeanor, and in all his utterances, mild and affectionate in his intercourse with his family, he seemed quite unconscious of the heroism he manifested in those achievements, which gave him ever increasing renown.

Life in the cabin of the frontiersman, where the wants are few, and the supplies abundant, is comparatively a leisure life. These men knew but little of the hurry and the bustle with which those in the crowded city engage daily in the almost deadly struggle for bread. There was no want in the cabin of Daniel Boone. As these two hardy adventurers, John Finley and Daniel Boone, sat together hour after hour by the fire, talking of the new country which Finley had explored, the hearts of both burned within them again to penetrate those remote realms. To them there were no hardships in the journey. At the close of each day's march, which but slightly wearied their toughened sinews, they could in a few moments throw up a shelter, beneath which they would enjoy more luxurious sleep than the traveler, after being rocked in the rail-cars, can now find on the softest couches of our metropolitan hotels. And the dainty morsel cut with artistic skill from the fat buffalo, and toasted on the end of a ramrod before the camp-fire, possessed a relish which few epicures have ever experienced at the most sumptuous tables in Paris or New York. And as these men seem to have been constitutionally devoid of any emotions of fear from wild beasts, or still wilder Indians, the idea of a journey of a few hundred miles in the wilderness was not one to be regarded by them with any special solicitude.

Gradually they formed a plan for organizing a small party to traverse these beautiful realms in search of a new home. A company of six picked men was formed, and Daniel Boone was chosen their leader. The names of this party were John Finley, John Stewart, Joseph Holden, James Moncey, and William Cool. A journey of many hundred miles was before them. Through the vast mountain barrier, which could only be traversed by circuitous wanderings some hundreds of miles in extent, their route was utterly pathless, and there were many broad and rapid streams to be crossed, which flowed through the valleys between the mountain ridges. Though provision in abundance was scattered along the way, strong clothing must be provided, powder and bullets they must take with them, and all these necessaries were to be carried upon their backs, for no pack horses could thread the defiles of the mountains or climb their rugged cliffs. It was also necessary to make provision for the support of the families of these adventurers during their absence of many months. It does not appear that Mrs. Boone presented any obstacle in the way of her husband's embarking in this adventure. Her sons were old enough to assist her in the management of the farm, and game was still to be found in profusion in the silent prairies and sublime forests which surrounded them.

In the sunny clime of North Carolina May comes with all the balminess and soft zephyrs of a more northern summer. It was a beautiful morning on the first day of May, 1769, when Boone and his companions commenced their adventurous journey. In the brief narrative which Boone has given of this excursion, we perceive that it was with some considerable regret that he separated himself from his much loved wife and children on the peaceful banks of the Yadkin.

We must infer that the first part of their journey was fatiguing, for it took them a full month to accomplish the passage of the mountains. Though it was less than a hundred miles across these ridges in a direct line, the circuitous route which it was necessary to take greatly lengthened the distance. And as they were never in a hurry, they would be very likely, when coming to one of the many lovely valleys on the banks of the Holstein, or the Clinch River, to be enticed to some days of delay. Where now there are thriving villages filled with the hum of the industries of a high civilization, there was then but the solitary landscape dotted with herds of buffalo and of deer.

Boone says that in many of these regions he found buffalo roving in companies of several hundreds feeding upon the tender leaves of the canebrake, or browsing upon the smooth and extended meadows. Being far removed from the usual route of the Indian hunters, they were very tame, manifesting no fear at the approach of man.

On the seventh of June, our adventurers, at the close of a day of arduous travel, reached an eminence of the Cumberland Mountains, which gave them a commanding and an almost entrancing view of the region beyond, now known as the State of Kentucky. At the height upon which they stood, the expanse spreading out to the West, until lost in the distant horizon, presented an aspect of nature's loveliness such as few eyes have ever beheld. The sun was brilliantly sinking, accompanied by a gorgeous retinue of clouds. Majestic forests, wide-spread prairies, and lakes and rivers, gilded by the setting sun, confirmed the truth of the most glowing reports which had been heard from the lips of Finley. An artist has seized upon this incident, which he has transferred to canvass, in a picture which he has entitled, "Daniel Boone's first view of Kentucky." Engravings have been so multiplied of this painting, that it has become familiar to most eyes.

The appearance of our adventurers is thus graphically described by Mr. Peck, in his excellent Life of Daniel Boone.

"Their dress was of the description usually worn at that period by all forest-rangers. The outside garment was a hunting shirt, or loose open frock, made of dressed deer-skins. Leggins, or drawers, of the same material, covered the lower extremities, to which was appended a pair of moccasins for the feet. The cape or collar of the hunting shirt, and the seams of the leggins were adorned with fringes. The undergarments were of coarse cotton. A leather belt encircled the body. On the right side was suspended the tomahawk, to be used as a hatchet. On the left was the hunting-knife, powder-horn, bullet-pouch, and other appendages indispensable for a hunter. Each person bore his trusty rifle, and as the party made its toilsome way amid the shrubs, and over the logs and loose shrubs, that accident had thrown upon the obscure trail they were following, each man gave a sharp lookout, as though danger, or a lurking enemy were near. Their garments were soiled and rent; the unavoidable result of long travel and exposure to the heavy rains which had fallen, the weather having been stormy and uncomfortable, and they had traversed a mountainous wilderness for several hundred miles. The leader of the party was of full size, with a hardy, robust, sinewy frame, and keen piercing hazel eyes, that glanced with quickness at every object as they passed on, now cast forward in the direction they were travelling, for signs of an old trail, and in the next moment directed askance into the dense forest or the deep ravine, as if watching some concealed enemy. The reader will recognise in this man, the pioneer Boone at the head of his companions."

The peculiar character of these men is developed in the fact, that, rapidly descending the western declivity of the mountains, they came to a beautiful meadow upon the banks of a little stream now called Red River. Here they reared their hut, and here they remained in apparently luxurious idleness all the summer; and here Daniel Boone remained all of the ensuing winter. Their object could scarcely have been to obtain furs, for they could not transport them across the mountains. There were in the vicinity quite a number of salt springs which the animals of the forest frequented in immense numbers. In the brief account which Boone gives of these long months, he simply says:

> "In this forest, the habitation of beasts of every kind natural to America, we practised hunting with great success until the twenty-second day of December following."

Bears, buffalo and deer were mainly the large game which fell before their rifles. Water-fowl, and also land birds of almost every variety, were found in great profusion. It must have been a strange life which these six men experienced during these seven months in the camp on the silent waters of the Red River. No Indians were seen, and no traces of them were discovered through this period. The hunters made several long excursions in various directions, apparently examining the country in reference to their own final settlement in it, and to the introduction of emigrants from the Atlantic border. Indeed it has been said that Daniel Boone was the secret agent of a company on the other side of the mountains, who wished to obtain possession of a large extent of territory for the formation of a colony there. But of this nothing with certainty is known. Yet there must have been some strong controlling motive to have induced these men to remain so long in their camp, which consisted simply of a shed of logs, on the banks of this solitary stream.

Three sides of the hut were enclosed. The interstices between the logs were filled with moss or clay. The roof was also carefully covered with bark, so as to be impervious to rain. The floor was spread over with dry leaves and with the fragrant twigs of the hemlock, presenting a very inviting couch for the repose of weary men. The skins of buffaloes and of bears presented ample covering for their night's repose. The front of the hut, facing the south, was entirely open, before which blazed their camp-fire. Here the men seem to have been very happy. The climate was mild; they were friendly to each other; they had good health and abundance of food was found in their camp.

On the twenty-second of December, Boone, with one of his companions, John Stewart, set out on one of their exploring tours. There were parts of the country called cane-brakes, covered with cane growing so thickly together as to be quite impenetrable to the hunter. Through portions of these the buffaloes had trampled their way in large companies, one following another, opening paths called *streets*. These streets had apparently been trodden for ages. Following these paths, Boone and his companion had advanced several miles from their camp, when suddenly a large party of Indians sprang from their concealment and seized them both as captives. The action was so sudden that there was no possibility of resistance. In the following words Boone describes this event:

> "This day John Stewart and I had a pleasing ramble, but fortune changed the scene in the close of it. We had passed through a great forest, on which stood myriads of trees, some gay with blossoms, others rich with fruits. Nature was here a series of wonders and a fund of delight. Here she displayed her ingenuity and industry in a variety of flowers and fruits, beautifully colored, elegantly shaped, and charmingly flavored; and we were diverted with innumerable animals presenting themselves perpetually to our view.
>
> "In the decline of the day, near Kentucky river, as we ascended the brow of a small hill, a number of Indians rushed out upon us from a thick canebrake and made us prisoners. The time of our sorrow was now arrived. They plundered us of what we had, and kept us in confinement seven days, treating us with common savage usage."

The peculiar character of Boone was here remarkably developed. His whole course of life had made him familiar with the manners and customs of the Indians. They were armed only with bows and arrows. He had the death-dealing rifle which they knew not how to use. His placid temper was never ruffled by elation in prosperity or despair in adversity. He assumed perfect contentment with his lot, cultivated friendly relations with them, taught them many things they did not know, and aided them in all the ways in his power. His rifle ball would instantly strike down the buffalo, when the arrow of the Indian would only goad him to frantic flight.

The Indians admired the courage of their captive, appreciated his skill, and began to regard him as a friend and a helper. They relaxed their vigilance, while every day they were leading their prisoners far away from their camp into the boundless West. Boone was so well acquainted with the Indian character as to be well aware that any attempt to escape, if unsuccessful, would cause his immediate death. The Indians, exasperated by what they would deem such an insult to their hospitality, would immediately bury the tomahawk in his brain. Thus seven days and nights passed away.

At the close of each day's travel the Indians selected some attractive spot for the night's encampment or bivouac, according to the state of the weather, near some spring or stream. Here they built a rousing fire, roasted choice cuts from the game they had taken, and feasted abundantly with jokes and laughter, and many boastful stories of their achievements. They then threw themselves upon the ground for sleep, though some one was appointed to keep a watch over their captives. But deceived by the entire contentment and friendliness, feigned by Boone, and by Stewart who implicitly followed the counsel of his leader's superior mind, all thoughts of any attempt of their captives to escape soon ceased to influence the savages.

On the seventh night after the capture, the Indians, gorged with an abundant feast, were all soundly asleep. It was midnight. The flickering fire burned feebly. The night was dark. They were in the midst of an apparently boundless forest. The favorable hour for an attempt to escape had come. But it was full of peril. Failure was certain death, for the Indians deemed it one of the greatest of all crimes for a captive who had been treated with kindness to attempt to escape. A group of fierce savages were sleeping around, each one of whom accustomed to midnight alarms, was supposed to sleep, to use an expressive phrase, "with one eye open." Boone, who had feigned sound slumber, cautiously awoke his companion who was asleep and motioned him to follow. The rustling of a leaf, the crackling of a twig, would instantly cause every savage to grasp his bow and arrow and spring from the ground. Fortunately the Indians had allowed their captives to retain their guns, which had proved so valuable in obtaining game.

With step as light as the fall of a feather these men with moccasined feet crept from the encampment. After a few moments of intense solicitude, they found themselves in the impenetrable gloom of the forest, and their captors still undisturbed. With vastly superior native powers to the Indian, and equally accustomed to forest life, Boone was in all respects their superior. With the instinct of the bee, he made a straight line towards the encampment they had left, with the locality of which the Indians were not acquainted. The peril which menaced them added wings to their flight. It was mid-winter, and though not very cold in that climate, fortunately for them, the December nights were long.

Six precious hours would pass before the dawn of the morning would struggle through the tree-tops. Till then the bewildered Indians could obtain no clue whatever to the direction of their flight. Carefully guarding against leaving any traces of their footsteps behind them, and watching with an eagle eye lest they should encounter any other band of savages, they pressed forward hour after hour with sinews apparently as tireless as if they had been wrought of iron. When the fugitives reached their camp they found it plundered and deserted. Whether the red men had discovered it and carried off their companions as prisoners, or whether the white men in a panic had destroyed what they could not remove and had attempted a retreat to the settlements, was never known. It is probable that in some way they perished in the wilderness, and that their fate is to be added to the thousands of tragedies occurring in this world which no pen has recorded.

The intrepid Boone and his companion Stewart seemed, however, to have no idea of abandoning their encampment. But apprehensive that the Indians might have discovered their retreat, they reared a small hut in another spot, still more secret and secure. It is difficult to imagine what motive could have led these two men to remain any longer in these solitudes, five hundred miles from home, exposed to so many privations and to such fearful peril. Notwithstanding the utmost care in husbanding their resources, their powder and lead were rapidly disappearing, and there was no more to be obtained in the wilderness. But here they remained a month, doing apparently nothing, but living luxuriously, according to their ideas of good cheer. The explanation is probably to be found in the fascination of this life of a hunter, which once enjoyed, seems almost irresistible, even to those accustomed to all the appliances of a high civilization.

A gentleman from New York, who spent a winter among the wild scenes of the Rocky Mountains, describes in the following graphic language, the effect of these scenes upon his own mind:

"When I turned my horse's head from Pikes Peak, I quite regretted the abandonment of my mountain life, solitary as it was, and more than once thought of again taking the trail to the Salado Valley, where I enjoyed such good sport. Apart from the feeling of loneliness, which anyone in my situation must naturally have experienced, surrounded by the stupendous works of nature, which in all their solitary grandeur frowned upon me, there was something inexpressibly exhilarating in the sensation of positive freedom from all worldly care, and a consequent expansion of the sinews, as it were, of mind and body, which made me feel elastic as a ball of india-rubber, and in such a state of perfect ease, that no more dread of scalping Indians entered my mind, than if I had been sitting in Broadway, in one of the windows of the Astor House.

"A citizen of the world, I never found any difficulty in investing my resting place wherever it might be, with the attributes of a home. Although liable to the accusation of barbarism, I must confess that the very happiest moments of my life have been spent in the wilderness of the Far West. I never recall but with pleasure the remembrance of my solitary camp in the Bayou Salado, with no friend near me more faithful than my rifle. With a plentiful supply of dry pine logs on the fire, and its cheerful blaze streaming far up into the sky, illuminating the valley far and near, I would sit enjoying the genial warmth, and watch the blue smoke as it curled upward, building castles in its vapory wreaths.

Scarcely did I ever wish to change such hours of freedom for all the luxuries of civilized life; and, unnatural and extraordinary as it may appear, yet such are the fascinations of the life of the mountain hunter, that I believe that not one instance could be adduced of even the most polished and civilized of men, who had once tasted the sweets of its attendant liberty, and freedom from every worldly care, not regretting to exchange them for the monotonous life of the settlements, and not sighing and sighing again for its pleasures and allurements.

"A hunter's camp in the Rocky Mountains, is quite a picture. It is invariably made in a picturesque locality, for, like the Indian, the white hunter has an eye to the beautiful. Nothing can be more social and cheering than the welcome blaze of the camp-fire on a cold winter's night, and nothing more amusing or entertaining, if not instructive, than the rough conversation of the simple-minded mountaineers, whose nearly daily task is all of exciting adventure, since their whole existence is spent in scenes of peril and privation. Consequently the narration is a tale of thrilling accidents, and hair-breadth escapes, which, though simple matter-of-fact to them, appears a startling romance to those unacquainted with the lives led by those men, who, with the sky for a roof, and their rifles to supply them with food and clothing, call no man lord or master, and are as free as the game they follow."

There are many events which occurred in the lives of Boone and his companions, which would seem absolutely incredible were they not sustained by evidence beyond dispute. Boone and Stewart were in a boundless, pathless, wilderness of forests, mountains, rivers and lakes. Their camp could not be reached from the settlements, but by a journey of many weeks, apparently without the smallest clue to its location. And yet the younger brother of Boone, upon whom had been conferred his father's singular baptismal name of Squire, set out with a companion to cross the mountains, in search of Daniel. One day in the latter part of January, Boone and Stewart were quite alarmed in seeing two men approach their camp. They supposed of course that they were Indians, and that they were probably followed by a numerous band. Escape was impossible. Captivity and death seemed certain. But to their surprise and delight, the two strangers proved to be white men; one the brother of Daniel Boone, and the other a North Carolinian who had accompanied him. They brought with them quite a supply of powder and lead; inestimable treasures in the remote wilderness. Daniel, in his Autobiography, in the following simple strain, alludes to this extraordinary occurrence:

> "About this time my brother Squire Boone, with another adventurer, who came to explore the country shortly after us, was wandering through the forest, determined to find me if possible, and accidentally found our camp. Notwithstanding the unfortunate circumstances of our company, and our dangerous situation as surrounded by hostile savages, our meeting so fortunately in the wilderness made us reciprocally sensible of the utmost satisfaction. So much does friendship triumph over misfortune, that sorrows and sufferings vanish at the meeting, not only of real friends, but of the most distant acquaintances, and substitute happiness in their room."

Our hardy pioneer, far more familiar with his rifle than his pen, comments as follows on their condition:

> "We were in a helpless, dangerous situation; exposed daily to perils and death, among savages and wild beasts. Not a white man in the country but ourselves. Thus situated, many hundred miles from our families, in the howling wilderness, I believe few would have equally enjoyed the happiness we experienced. I often observed to my brother, 'You see how little nature requires to be satisfied. Felicity, the companion of content, is rather found in our own breasts, than in the enjoyment of external things; and I firmly believe it requires but a little philosophy to make a man happy in whatsoever state he is. This consists in a full resignation to the will of Providence; and a resigned soul finds pleasure in a path strewed with briers and thorns.'"

Chapter 5

INDIAN WARFARE

The valley of the Clinch River is but one of the many magnificent ravines amid the gigantic ranges of the Alleghany mountains. Boone, speaking of these ridges which he so often had occasion to cross, says:

> "These mountains in the wilderness, as we pass from the old settlements in Virginia to Kentucky, are ranged in a south-west and north-east direction and are of great length and breadth and not far distant from each other. Over them nature hath formed passes that are less difficult than might be expected from a view of such huge piles. The aspect of these cliffs is so wild and horrid that it is impossible to behold them without terror. The spectator is apt to imagine that nature has formerly suffered some violent convulsion, and that these are the dismembered remains of the dreadful shock."

One cannot but regret that no memorials are left of a wonderful journey, full of romantic interest and exciting adventure, which Boone at one time took to the Falls of the Ohio, to warn some surveyors of their danger. He reached them in safety, rescued them from certain death, and conducted them triumphantly back to the settlements. So long as the white men, with their rifles, could keep upon the open prairie, they could defend themselves from almost any number of Indians, who could only assail them with bows and arrows. But the moment they entered the forest, or any ravine among the hills, the little band was liable to hear the war-whoop of a thousand Indian braves in the ambush around, and to be assailed by a storm of arrows and javelins from unseen hands.

A few days after Boone's arrival at the encampment near the Falls of the Ohio, and as the surveyors were breaking camp in preparation for their precipitate retreat, several of their number who had gone to a spring at a short distance from the camp, were suddenly attacked on the twentieth of July by a large party of Indians. One was instantly killed. The rest being nearly surrounded, fled as best they could in all directions. One man hotly pursued, rushed along an Indian trail till he reached the Ohio River. Here he chanced to find a bark canoe. He jumped into it and pushed out into the rapid stream till beyond the reach of the Indian arrows. The swift current bore him down the river, by curves and head-lands, till he was far beyond the encampment.

To return against the strong flood, with the savages watching for him, seemed perilous, if not impossible. It is said that he floated down the whole length of the Ohio and of the Mississippi, a distance not less probably, counting the curvatures of the stream, than two thousand miles, and finally found his way by sea to Philadelphia, probably in some vessel which he encountered near the coast. This is certainly one of the most extraordinary voyages which ever occurred. It was mid-summer, so that he could not suffer from cold. Grapes often hung in rich clusters in the forests, which lined the river banks, and various kinds of nutritious berries were easily gathered to satisfy hunger.

As these men never went into the forest without the rifle and a supply of ammunition, and as they never lost a bullet by an inaccurate shot, it is not probable that our adventurer suffered from hunger. But the incidents of such a voyage must have been so wonderful, that it is greatly to be regretted that we have no record of them.

The apprehensions of Lord Dunmore, respecting the conspiracy of the Indians, proved to have been well founded. Though Boone, with his great sagacity, led his little band by safe paths back to the settlements, a very fierce warfare immediately blazed forth all along the Virginia frontier. This conflict with the Indians, very brief and very bloody, is usually called Lord Dunmore's war. The white men have told the story, and they admit that the war "arose in consequence of cold-blooded murders committed upon inoffensive Indians in the region of the upper Ohio."

One of the provocatives to this war was the assassination by fiendlike white men of the whole family of the renowned Indian chief, Logan, in the vicinity of the city of Wheeling. Logan had been the friend of the white man. But exasperated by these outrages, he seized his tomahawk breathing only vengeance. General Gibson was sent to one of the Shawanese towns to confer with Logan and to detach him from the conspiracy against the whites. It was on this occasion that Logan made that celebrated speech whose pathetic eloquence will ever move the human heart:

> "I appeal to any white man to say if ever he entered Logan's cabin hungry, and I gave him not meat; if ever he came cold or naked and I gave him not clothing. During the course of the last long and bloody war, Logan remained in his tent, an advocate of peace. Nay, such was my love for the whites, that those of my own country pointed at me and said, 'Logan is the friend of white men.' I had even thought to live with you, but for the injuries of one man. Colonel Cresap, the last spring, in cool

blood and unprovoked, cut off all the relatives of Logan, not sparing even my women and children. There runs not a drop of my blood in the veins of any human creature. This called on me for revenge. I have killed many. I have fully glutted my vengeance. For my country, I rejoice at the beams of peace. Yet do not harbor the thought that mine is the joy of fear. Logan never felt fear. He will not turn on his heel to save his life. Who is there to mourn for Logan?"

This war, though it lasted but a few months, was very sanguinary. Every exposed point on the extensive Virginia frontier was assailed. Cabins were burned, harvests were trampled down, cattle driven off, and men, women, and children either butchered or carried into captivity more dreadful than death. The peril was so dreadful that the most extraordinary efforts on the part of the Virginian Government were requisite to meet it. An army of three thousand men was raised in the utmost haste. This force was in two divisions. One of eleven hundred men rendezvoused in what is now Green Briar county, and marched down the valley of the Great Kanawha, to its entrance into the Ohio, at a place now named Point Pleasant.

Lord Dunmore with the remaining nineteen hundred crossed the Cumberland Mountains to Wheeling, and thence descended the Ohio in boats, to form a junction with the other party at the mouth of the Great Kanawha. Thence united, they were to march across the country about forty miles due west, to the valley of the Scioto. The banks of this lovely stream were lined with Indian villages, in a high state of prosperity. Corn-fields waved luxuriantly around their humble dwellings. They were living at peace with each other, and relied far more upon the produce of the soil, than upon the chase, for their support.

It was the plan of Lord Dunmore to sweep this whole region with utter desolation, and entirely to exterminate the Indians. But the savages did not await his arrival in their own homes. Many of them had obtained guns and ammunition from the French in Canada, with whom they seem to have lived on the most friendly terms.

In a well-ordered army for Indian warfare, whose numbers cannot now with certainty be known, they crossed the Ohio, below the mouth of the

Great Kanawha, and marching through the forest, in the rear of the hills, fell by surprise very impetuously upon the rear of the encampment at Point Pleasant. The Indians seemed to be fully aware that their only safety was in the energies of desperation. One of the most bloody battles was then fought, which ever occurred in Indian warfare. Though the Virginians with far more potent weapons repelled their assailants, they paid dearly for their victory. Two hundred and fifteen of the Virginians fell dead or severely wounded beneath the bullets or arrows of their foes. The loss which the savages incurred could never be ascertained with accuracy. It was generally believed that several hundred of their warriors were struck down on that bloody field.

The whites, accustomed to Indian warfare and skilled in the use of the rifle, scarcely fired a shot which did not reach its mark. In the cautious warfare between the tribes, fighting with arrows from behind trees, the loss of fifteen or twenty warriors was deemed a great calamity. Now, to find hundreds of their braves weltering in blood, was awful beyond precedent, and gave them new ideas of the prowess of the white man. In this conflict the Indians manifested a very considerable degree of military ability. Having constructed a breastwork of logs, behind which they could retreat in case of a repulse, they formed in a long line extending across the point from the Kanawha to the Ohio. Then they advanced in the impetuous attack through the forest, protected by logs, and stumps, and trees. Had they succeeded in their assault, there would have been no possible escape for the Virginian troops. They must have been annihilated.

The Indians had assembled on that field nearly all the warriors of four powerful tribes; the Shawnee, Delaware, Mingo and Wyandotts. After the repulse, panic-stricken, they fled through the wilderness, unable to make any other stand against their foes. Lord Dunmore, with his triumphant army flushed with victory and maddened by its serious loss, marched rapidly down the left bank of the Ohio, and then crossed into the valley of the Scioto to sweep it with flame. We have no account of the details of this cruel expedition, but the following graphic description of a similar excursion into the land belonging to the Cherokees, will give one a vivid idea of the nature of these conflicts.

The celebrated Francis Marion, who was an officer in the campaign, and an eye-witness of the scenes which he describes, gives the following narrative of the events which ensued:

"Now commenced a scene of devastation scarcely paralleled in the annals of this continent. For thirty days the army employed themselves in burning and ravaging the settlements of the broken-spirited Indians. No less than fourteen of their towns were laid in ashes; their granaries were yielded to the flames, their corn-fields ravaged, while the miserable fugitives, flying from the sword, took refuge with their starving families among the mountains. As the lands were rich and the season had been favorable, the corn was bending under the double weight of lusty roasting ears and pods and clustering beans. The furrows seemed to rejoice under their precious loads. The fields stood thick with bread. We encamped the first night in the woods near the fields where the whole army feasted on the young corn, which, with fat venison, made a most delicious treat. The next morning, by order of Col. Grant, we proceeded to burn down the Indian cabins.

"Some of our men seemed to enjoy this cruel work, laughing very heartily at the curling flames as they mounted loud crackling over the tops of the huts. But to me it appeared a shocking sight. 'Poor creatures!' thought I, 'we surely need not grudge you such miserable habitations.' But when we came according to orders to cut down the fields of corn, I could scarcely refrain from tears; for who could see the stalks that stood so stately, with broad green leaves and gaily tasseled shocks, filled with the sweet milky flour, the staff of life,—who, I say, could see without grief these sacred plants sinking under our swords with all their precious load, to wither and rot untasted in the fields.

"I saw everywhere around the footsteps of little Indian children, where they had lately played under shelter of the rustling corn. No doubt they had often looked up with joy to the swelling shocks, and were gladdened when they thought of the abundant cakes for the coming winter. 'When we are gone,' thought I, 'they will return, and peeping through the weeds, with tearful eyes, will mark the ghastly ruin poured over their homes and the happy fields where they had so often played.'"

Such was life among the comparatively intelligent tribes in the beautiful and fertile valley of the Scioto. Such was the scene of devastation, or of "punishing the Indians," as it was called, upon which Lord Dunmore's army entered, intending to sweep the valley with fire and sword from its opening at the Ohio to its head waters leagues away in the North.

In this campaign the Indians, while with much sagacity they combined their main force to encounter the army under Lord Dunmore, detached separate bands of picked warriors to assail the settlements on the frontier at every exposed point. These bands of painted savages, emerging from the solitudes of the forests at midnight, would fall with hideous yells upon the lone cabin of the settler, or upon a little cluster of log huts, and in a few hours nothing would be left but smouldering ruins and gory corpses.

To Daniel Boone, who had manifested wonderful skill in baffling all the stratagems of Indian warfare, was assigned the difficult and infinitely important task of protecting these frontiers. Three garrisons were placed under his command, over which he exercised supreme control. He located them at the most available points; noiselessly passed from one to the other to see that they were fortified according to the most approved principles of military engineering then known in the forest. His scouts were everywhere, to give prompt notice of any approach of hostile bands. Thus this quiet, silent man, with great efficiency, fulfilled his mission to universal satisfaction. Without seeking fame, without thinking even of such a reward for his services, his sagacity and his virtues were rapidly giving him a very enviable reputation throughout all those regions.

The discomfited Indians had become thoroughly disheartened, and sent couriers to Lord Dunmore imploring peace. Comstock, their chief, seems to have been a man not only of strong native powers of mind, but of unusual intelligence. With quite a brilliant retinue of his warriors, he met Lord Dunmore in council at a point in the valley of the Scioto, about four miles south of the present city of Circleville. Comstock himself opened the deliberations with a speech of great dignity and argumentative power. In a loud voice, which was heard, as he intended, by all in the camp, he portrayed the former prosperous condition of the Indian tribes, powerful in numbers and abounding in wealth, in the enjoyment of their rich cornfields, and their forests filled with game. With this he contrasted very forcibly their present wretched condition, with diminished numbers, and with the loss of their hunting grounds. He reproached the whites with the violation of their treaty obligations, and declared that the Indians had been forbearing in the extreme under the wrongs which had been inflicted upon them.

"We know," said he, "perfectly well, our weakness when compared with the English. The Indians desire only justice. The war was not sought by us, but was forced upon us. It was commenced by the whites. We should have merited the contempt of every white man could we have tamely submitted to the murders which have been inflicted upon our unoffending people at the hands of the white men."

The power was with Lord Dunmore. In the treaty of peace he exacted terms which, though very hard for the Indians, were perhaps not more than he had a right to require. The Indians surrendered four of their principal warriors as hostages for the faithful observance of the treaty. They relinquished all claims whatever to the vast hunting grounds which their bands from time immemorial had ranged south of the Ohio River. This was an immense concession. Lord Dunmore returned across the mountains well satisfied with his campaign, though his soldiers were excited almost to mutiny in not being permitted to wreak their vengeance upon the unhappy savages.

And here let it be remarked, that deeply wronged as these Indians unquestionably were, there was not a little excuse for the exasperation of the whites. Fiends incarnate could not have invented more terrible tortures than they often inflicted upon their captives. We have no heart to describe these scenes. They are too awful to be contemplated. In view of the horrid barbarity thus practised, it is not strange that the English should have wished to shoot down the whole race, men, women, and children, as they would exterminate wolves or bears.

This campaign being thus successfully terminated, Daniel Boone returned to his humble cabin on the Clinch River. Here he had a small and fertile farm, which his energetic family had successfully cultivated during the summer, and he spent the winter months in his favorite occupation of hunting in the forests around. His thoughtful mind, during these long and solitary rambles, was undoubtedly occupied with plans for the future. Emigration to his beautiful Kentucky was still his engrossing thought.

It is not wonderful that a man of such fearless temperament, and a natural turn of mind so poetic and imaginative, should have been charmed beyond expression by a realm whose attractions he had so fully experienced. That the glowing descriptions of Boone and Finley were not exaggerated, is manifest from the equally rapturous account of others who now began to explore this favored land. Imlay writes of that region:

> "Everything here assumes a dignity and splendor I have never seen in any other part of the world. You ascend a considerable distance from the shores of the Ohio, and when you would suppose you had arrived at the summit of a mountain, you find yourself upon an extensive level. Here an eternal verdure reigns, and the brilliant sun of latitude 39 degrees, piercing through the azure heavens, produces in this prolific soil an early maturity which is truly astonishing. Flowers full and perfect, as if they had been cultivated by the hand of a florist, with all their captivating odors, and with all the variegated charms which color and nature can produce, here in the lap of elegance and beauty, decorate the smiling groves. Soft zephyrs gently breathe on sweets, and the inhaled air gives a glow of health and vigor that seems to ravish the intoxicated senses."

The Virginian government now resolved to pour a tide of emigration into these as yet unexplored realms, south of the Ohio. Four hundred acres of land were offered to every individual who would build a cabin, clear a lot of land, and raise a crop of corn. This was called a settlement right. It was not stated how large the clearing should be, or how extensive the cornfield. Several settlements were thus begun in Kentucky, when there was a new and extraordinary movement which attracted universal attention.

A very remarkable man, named Richard Henderson, appeared in North Carolina. Emerging from the humblest walks of life, and unable even to read until he had obtained maturity, he developed powers of conversational eloquence and administrative ability of the highest order.

The Cherokee Indians claimed the whole country bounded by the Kentucky, the Ohio, and the Cumberland rivers, and we know not how much more territory extending indefinitely to the South and West. Colonel Henderson formed an association of gentlemen, which he called the Transylvania Company. Making a secret journey to the Cherokee country, he met twelve hundred chiefs in council, and purchased of them the whole territory, equal to some European kingdoms, bounded by the above mentioned rivers. For this realm, above a hundred miles square, he paid the insignificant sum of ten wagon loads of cheap goods, with a few fire-arms and some spirituous liquors.

Mr. Henderson, to whom the rest of the company seemed to have delegated all their powers, now assumed the position of proprietor, governor, and legislator of his magnificent domain, which he called Transylvania. It seems that Boone accompanied Colonel Henderson to the council of the Cherokee chieftains which was held at Wataga, the southern branch of the Holston River. Boone had explored nearly the whole of this region, and it was upon his testimony that the company relied in endeavoring to purchase these rich and fertile lands. Indeed, as we have before intimated, it has been said that Boone in his wonderful and perilous explorations was the agent of this secret company.

No treaties with the Indians were sure of general acquiescence. There were always discontented chieftains; there were almost always conflicting claims of hostile tribes; there were always wandering tribes of hunters and of warriors, who, exasperated by the treatment which they had received from vagabond white men, were ever ready to wreak their vengeance upon any band of emigrants they might encounter.

Colonel Henderson's treaty was made in the month of March, 1775. With characteristic vigor, he immediately made preparations for the settlement of the kingdom of which he was the proud monarch. The first thing to be done was to mark out a feasible path through which emigrants might pass, without losing their way, over the mountains and through the wilderness, to the heart of this new Eden. Of all the men in the world, Daniel Boone was the one to map out this route of five hundred miles. He took with him a company of road-makers, and in a few months opened a path which could be traversed by pack-horses, and even by wagons to a place called Boonesville on the Kentucky River, within about thirty miles of the present site of Lexington.

The Indian hunters and warriors, notwithstanding the treaties into which the chieftains of the North and the South had entered, watched the construction of this road with great solicitude. They knew full well that it would ere long secure their expulsion from their ancient hunting grounds. Though no general warfare was organized by the tribes, it was necessary to be constantly on the watch against lawless bands, who were determined to harass the pioneers in every possible way. In the following letter Boone communicated to Colonel Henderson the hostility which they had, perhaps unexpectedly, encountered. It was dated the first of April, and was sent back by a courier through the woods:

"Dear Colonel,—
"After my compliments to you, I shall acquaint you with my misfortunes. On March the Twenty-fifth, a party of Indians fired on my company about half an hour before day, and killed Mr. Twitty and his negro, and wounded Mr. Walker very deeply; but I hope he will recover. On March the Twenty-eighth, as we were hunting for provisions, we found Samuel Tale's son who gave us an account that the Indians fired on their camp on the twenty-seventh day. My brother and I went down and found two men killed and scalped, Thomas McDowell and Jeremiah McPeters. I have sent a man down to all the lower companies, in order to gather them all to the mouth of the Otter Creek. My advice to you, sir, is to come or send as soon as possible. Your company is desired greatly, for the people are very uneasy, but are willing to stay and venture their lives with you. And now is the time to frustrate their (the Indians) intentions, and keep the country while we are in it. If we give way to them now, it will ever be the case. This day we start from the battle ground to the mouth of Otter Creek, where we shall immediately erect a fort, which will be done before you can come or send. Then we can send ten men to meet you, if you send for them.
"I am, Sir, your most obedient servant,
"Daniel Boone."

Boone immediately commenced upon the left bank of the Kentucky River, which here ran in a westerly direction, the erection of a fort. Their position was full of peril, for the road-makers were but few in number, and Indian warriors to the number of many hundreds might at any time encircle them. Many of these Indians had also obtained muskets from the French in Canada, and had become practiced marksmen. Nearly three months were busily occupied in the construction of this important fort. Fortunately we have a minute description of its structure, and a sketch of its appearance, either from the pencil of Colonel Henderson, or of someone in his employ.

The fort or fortress consisted of a series of strong log huts, enclosing a large interior or square. The parallelogram was about two hundred and sixty feet in length and one hundred and fifty in breadth. These cabins, built of logs, were bullet-proof. The intervals between them were filled with stout pieces of timber, about twelve feet high, planted firmly in the ground, in close contact with each other, and sharpened at the top. The fort was built close to the river, with one of its angles almost overhanging the water, so that an abundant supply could be obtained without peril. Each of the corner houses projected a little, so that from the port-holes any Indian could be shot who should approach the walls with ladder or hatchet. This really artistic structure was not completed until the fourteenth day of June. The Indians from a distance watched its progress with dismay. They made one attack, but were easily repelled, though they succeeded in shooting one of the emigrants.

Daniel Boone contemplated the fortress on its completion with much satisfaction. He was fully assured that behind its walls and palisades bold hearts, with an ample supply of ammunition, could repel any assaults which the Indians were capable of making. He now resolved immediately to return to Clinch River, and bring his family out to share with him his new and attractive home.

Chapter 6

SUFFERINGS OF THE PIONEERS

The fortress at Boonesborough consisted of ten strong log huts arranged in a quadrangular form, enclosing an area of about one-third of an acre. The intervals, as before stated, between the huts, were filled with strong palisades of timber, which, like the huts themselves, were bullet-proof. The outer sides of the cabins, together with the palisades, formed the sides of the fort exposed to the foe. Each of these cabins was about twenty feet in length and twelve or fifteen in breadth. There were two entrance gates opposite each other, made of thick slabs of timber, and hung on wooden hinges. The forest, which was quite dense, had been cut away to such a distance as to expose an assailing party to the bullets of the garrison. As at that time the Indians were armed mainly with bows and arrows, a few men fully supplied with ammunition within the fort could bid defiance to almost any number of savages. And subsequently, as the Indians obtained fire-arms, they could not hope to capture the fort without a long siege, or by assailing it with a vastly overwhelming superiority of numbers. The accompanying illustration will give the reader a very correct idea of this renowned fortress of logs, which was regarded as the Gibraltar of Indian warfare.

Having finished this fort Daniel Boone, leaving a sufficient garrison for its security, set out for his home on the Clinch River to bring his wife and family to the beautiful land he so long had coveted for their residence. It seems that his wife and daughters were eager to follow their father to the banks of the Kentucky, whose charms he had so glowingly described to them. Several other families were also induced to join the party of emigration. They could dwell together in a very social community and in perfect safety in the spacious cabins within the fortress. The river would furnish them with an unfailing supply of water. The hunters, with their rifles, could supply them with game, and with those rifles could protect themselves while laboring in the fields, which with the axe they had laid open to the sun around the fort. The hunters and the farmers at night returning within the enclosure, felt perfectly safe from all assaults.

Daniel Boone commenced his journey with his wife and children, and others who joined them, back to Boonesborough in high spirits. It was a long journey of several hundred miles, and to many persons it would seem a journey fraught with great peril, for they were in danger almost every mile of the way, of encountering hostile Indians. But Boone, accustomed to traversing the wilderness, and accompanied by well-armed men, felt no more apprehensions of danger than the father of a family would at the present day in traveling by cars from Massachusetts to Pennsylvania.

It was beautiful autumnal weather when the party of pioneers commenced its adventurous tour through the wilderness, to find a new home five hundred miles beyond even the remotest frontiers of civilization. There were three families besides that of Boone, and numbered in all twenty-six men, four women, and four or five boys and girls of various ages. Daniel Boone was the happy leader of this heroic little band.

In due time they all arrived safely at Boonesborough "without having encountered," as Boone writes, "any other difficulties than such as are common to this passage." As they approached the fort, Boone and his family, for some unexplained reason, pressed forward, and entered the fortress a few days in advance of the rest of the party. Perhaps Boone himself had a little pride to have it said, that Mrs. Boone and her daughter were the first of her color and sex that ever stood upon the banks of the wild and beautiful Kentucky.

A few days after their arrival, the emigrants had a very solemn admonition of the peril which surrounded them, and of the necessity of constant vigilance to guard against a treacherous and sleepless foe. One of their number who had sauntered but a short distance from the fort, lured by the combined beauty of the field, the forest and the river, was shot by a prowling Indian, who, raising the war-whoop of exultation and defiance, immediately disappeared in the depths of the wilderness.

Colonel Henderson and his partners, anxious to promote the settlement of the country, by organising parties of emigration, were busy in making known through the settlements the absolute security of the fort at Boonesborough, and the wonderful attractions of the region, in soil, climate, and abounding game. Henderson himself soon started with a large party, forty of whom were well armed. A number of pack-horses conveyed the luggage of the emigrants. Following the very imperfect road that Boone with much skill had engineered, which was quite tolerable for pack-horses in single file, they reached Boonesborough early in the following spring.

The Transylvania Company was in the full flush of successful experiment. Small parties of emigrants were constantly arriving. Boonesborough was the capital of the colony. Various small settlements were settled in its vicinity. Colonel Henderson opened a land office there, and in the course of a few months, over half a million of acres were entered, by settlers or speculators. These men did not purchase the lands outright, but bound themselves to pay a small but perpetual rent. The titles, which they supposed to be perfectly good, were given in the name of the "proprietors of the Colony of Transylvania, in America."

Soon four settlements were organised called Boonesborough, Harrodsburg, Boiling Spring, and St. Asaph. Colonel Henderson, on the twenty-third of May, 1775, as president or rather sovereign of this extraordinary realm, summoned a legislature consisting of delegates from this handful of pioneers, to meet at his capital, Boonesborough. Henderson presided. Daniel and his brother Squire were delegates from Boonesborough. A clergyman, the Reverend John Leythe, opened the session with prayer. Colonel Henderson made a remarkable and admirable speech. This extraordinary legislature represented only a constituency of one hundred and fifty souls. But the Colonel presented to them very clearly the true republican principle of government. He declared that the only legitimate source of political power is to be found in the will of the people, and added:

> "If any doubts remain among you with respect to the force and efficiency of whatever laws you now or hereafter make, be pleased to consider that all power is originally in the people. Make it their interest, therefore, by impartial and beneficent laws, and you may be sure of their inclination to see them enforced."

Rumors of these extraordinary proceedings reached the ears of Lord Dunmore. He considered the whole region of Kentucky as included in the original grant of Virginia, and that the Government of Virginia alone had the right to extinguish the Indian title to any of those lands. He therefore issued a proclamation, denouncing in the severest terms the "unlawful proceedings of one Richard Henderson and other disorderly persons, his associates." The legislature continued in session but three days, and honored itself greatly by its energetic action, and by the character of the laws which it inaugurated. One bill was introduced for preserving game; another for improving the breed of their horses; and it is worthy of especial record that a law was passed prohibiting profane swearing and Sabbath breaking.

The moral sense of these bold pioneers was shocked at the desecration of the Creator's name among their sublime solitudes.

The controversy between the Transylvania Company and the Government of Virginia was short but very sharp. Virginia could then very easily send an army of several thousand men to exterminate the Kentucky colony. A compromise was the result. The title of Henderson was declared "null and void." But he received in compensation a grant of land on the Ohio, about twelve miles square, below the mouth of Green River. Virginia assumed that the Indian title was entirely extinguished, and the region called Transylvania now belonged without encumbrance to the Old Dominion.

Still the tide of emigration continued to flow into this beautiful region. Among others came the family of Colonel Calloway, consisting of his wife and two daughters. For a long time no Indians had been seen in the vicinity of Boonesborough. No one seemed to apprehend the least danger from them, and the people in the fort wandered about as freely as if no foe had ever excited their fears. An accident occurred which sent a tremor of dismay through the whole colony, and which we will describe as related to the intelligent historian, Peck, from the lips of one of the parties, who experienced all the terrors of the scene:

"On the fourteenth of July, 1776, Betsey Calloway, her sister Frances, and Jemima Boone, a daughter of Daniel Boone, the two last about fourteen years of age, carelessly crossed the river opposite Boonesborough in a canoe, at a late hour in the afternoon. The trees and shrubs on the opposite bank were thick, and came down to the water's edge. The girls, unconscious of danger, were playing and splashing the water with their paddles, until the canoe floating with the current, drifted near the shore. Five stout Indians lay there concealed, one of whom, noiseless and stealthy as the serpent, crawled down the bank until he reached the rope that hung from the bow, turned its course up the stream, and in a direction to be hidden from the view of the fort. The loud shrieks of the captured girls were heard, but too late for their rescue.

"The canoe, their only means of crossing, was on the opposite shore, and none dared to risk the chance of swimming the river, under the impression that a large body of savages was concealed in the woods. Boone and Calloway were both absent, and night came on before arrangements could be made for their pursuit. Next morning by daylight we were on the track, and found they had prevented our following them by walking some distance apart through the thickest canes they could find. We observed their course, and on which side they had left their sign and traveled upwards of thirty miles. We then imagined they would be less cautious in traveling, and made a turn in order to cross their trace, and had gone but a few miles when we found their tracks in a buffalo path. We pursued and overtook them on going about ten miles, as they were kindling a fire to cook.

"Our study had been more to get the prisoners without giving the Indians time to murder them, after they discovered us, than to kill them. We discovered each other nearly at the same time. Four of us fired, and all of us rushed on them, which prevented them from carrying away anything, except one shot-gun without ammunition. Mr. Boone and myself had a pretty fair shoot, just as they began to move off. I am well convinced I shot one through, and the one he shot dropped his gun. Mine had none. The place was very thick with canes, and being so much elated on recovering the three broken-hearted girls, prevented our making further search. We sent them off without their mocassins, and not one of them with so much as a knife or a tomahawk."

The Indians seemed to awake increasingly to the consciousness that the empire of the white man in their country could only exist upon the ruins of their own. They divided themselves into several parties, making incessant attacks upon the forts, and prowling around to shoot every white man who could be found within reach of their bullets. They avoided all open warfare, and fought only when they could spring from an ambush, or when protected by a stump, a rock, or a tree. An Indian would conceal himself in the night behind a stump, shoot the first one who emerged from the fort in the morning, and then with a yell disappear in the recesses of the forest. The cattle could scarcely appear for an hour to graze beyond the protection of the fort, without danger of being struck down by the bullet of an unseen foe.

The war of the American Revolution was just commencing. Dreadfully it added to the perils of these distant emigrants. The British Government, with infamy which can never be effaced from her records, called in to her aid the tomahawk and the scalping knife of the savage. The Indian alone in his wild and merciless barbarity, was terrible enough. But when he appeared as the ally of a powerful nation, guided in his operations by the wisdom of her officers, and well provided with guns, powder, and bullets from inexhaustible resources, the settler had indeed reason to tremble. The winter of 1776 and 1777 was gloomy beyond expression. The Indians were hourly becoming more bold. Their predatory bands were wandering in all directions, and almost every day came fraught with tidings of outrage or massacre.

The whole military force of the colony was but about one hundred men. Three hundred of the pioneers, dismayed by the cloud of menace, every hour growing blacker, had returned across the mountains. There were but twenty-two armed men left in the fort at Boonesborough. The dismal winter passed slowly away, and the spring opened replete with nature's bloom and beauty, but darkened by the depravity of man. On the fifteenth of April, a band of a hundred howling Indians appeared in the forest before Boonesborough. With far more than their ordinary audacity, they rushed from their covert upon the fort. Had they been acquainted with the use of scaling ladders, by attacking at different points, they might easily, by their superior numbers, have carried the place by storm.

But fortunately the savages had but little military science, and when once repulsed, would usually retreat in dismay. The garrison, behind their impenetrable logs, took deliberate aim, and every bullet killed or wounded some Indian warrior. The savages fought with great bravery, and succeeded in killing one man in the garrison. Dismayed by the slaughter which they were encountering, they fled, taking their dead and wounded with them. But so fully were they conscious, that would they retain their own supremacy in the wilderness, they must exterminate the white man, that their retreat was only in preparation for a return with accumulated numbers.

An intelligent historian writes:

> "Daniel Boone appears before us in these exciting times the central figure towering like a colossus amid that hardy band of pioneers who opposed their breasts to the shock of the struggle which gave a terrible significance and a crimson hue to the history of the old dark and bloody ground."

The Indians were scattered everywhere in desperate bands. Forty men were sent from North Carolina and a hundred from Virginia, under Colonel Bowman, to strengthen the feeble settlements. The latter party arrived on the twentieth of August, 1776. There were at that time skirmishes with the Indians almost every day at some point. The pioneers within their log-houses, or behind their palisades, generally repelled these assaults with but little loss to themselves and not often inflicting severe injury to the wary savages. In the midst of these constant conflicts and dangers, the winter months passed drearily away. Boonesborough was constantly menaced and frequently attacked. In a diary kept within the fort we find the following entries:

> "*May 23.*—A large party of Indians attacked Boonesborough fort. Kept a warm fire till eleven o'clock at night. Began it next morning, and kept a warm fire till midnight. Attempting several times to burn the fort. Three of our men were wounded, but not mortally.
> "*May 26th.*—A party went out to hunt Indians. One wounded Squire Boone, and escaped."

Very cruel warfare was now being waged by the majestic power of Great Britain to bring the revolted colonies back to subjection to their laws. As we have mentioned they called into requisition on their side the merciless energies of the savage, openly declaring to the world that they were justified in making use of whatever weapons God and nature might place in their hands. From the strong British garrisons at Detroit, Vincennes and Kaskaskia, the Indians were abundantly supplied with rifles, powder and bullets, and were offered liberal rewards for such prisoners, and even scalps, as they might bring in.

The danger which threatened these settlements in Kentucky was now such as might cause the stoutest heart to quail. The savage had been adopted as an ally by the most wealthy and powerful nation upon the globe. His marauding bands were often guided by the intelligence of British officers. Boone organized what might be called a corps of explorers to go out two and two, penetrating the wilderness with extreme caution, in all directions, to detect any indication of the approach of the Indians. One of these explorers, Simon Kenton, acting under the sagacious counsel of Colonel Boone, had obtained great and deserved celebrity as among the most heroic of the remarkable men who laid the foundation of the State of Kentucky. It would be difficult to find in any pages of romance incidents of more wonderful adventure, or of more dreadful suffering, or stories of more miraculous escape, than were experienced by this man. Several times he was taken captive by the Indians, and though treated with great inhumanity, succeeded in making his escape. The following incident in his life, occurring about this time, gives one a very vivid picture of the nature of this warfare with the Indians:

> "Colonel Bowman sent Simon Kenton with two other men, Montgomery and Clark, on an exploring tour. Approaching an Indian town very cautiously in the night, on the north side of the Ohio River, they found a number of Indian horses in an enclosure. A horse in the wilderness was one of the most valuable of prizes. They accordingly each mounted an animal, and not daring to leave any behind, which would aid the Indians to pursue them, by hastily constructed halters they led the rest. The noise which the horses made awoke the Indians, and the whole village was at once in a state of uproar. The mounted adventurers dashed through the woods and were soon beyond the reach of the shouts and the yells which they left behind them. They knew, however, full well that the swift-footed Indian warriors would be immediately on their trail. Without a moment's rest they rode all night, the next day and the next night, and

on the morning of the second day reached the banks of the Ohio River. The flood of that majestic stream flowed broad and deep before them, and its surface was lashed into waves by a very boisterous wind. The horses could not swim across in such a gale, but their desire to retain the invaluable animals was so great that they resolved to wait upon the banks until sunset, when they expected the wind to abate. Having been so well mounted and having such a start of the Indians, they did not suppose it possible that their pursuers could overtake them before that time.

"Night came, but with it an increase of the fury of the gale, and the stream became utterly impassable. Early in the morning Kenton, who was separated from his companions, observed three Indians and a white man, well mounted, rapidly approaching. Raising his rifle, he took steady aim at the breast of the foremost Indian, and pulled the trigger. The powder flashed in the pan. Kenton took to his heels, but was soon overtaken and captured. The Indians seemed greatly exasperated at the loss of their horses. One seized him by the hair and shook his head 'till his teeth rattled.' The others scourged him severely with their ramrods over the head and face, exclaiming at every blow, 'Steal Indian hoss, hey!'

"Just then Kenton saw Montgomery coming boldly to his assistance. Instantly two Indian rifles were discharged, and Montgomery fell dead. His bloody scalp was waved in the face of Kenton, with menaces of a similar fate. Clark had sought safety in flight. Kenton was thrown upon the ground upon his back. His neck was fastened by a halter to a sapling; his arms, extended to their full length, were pinioned to the earth by stakes; his feet were fastened in a similar manner. A stout stick was passed across his breast, and so attached to the earth that he could not move his body. All this was done in the most violent and cruel manner, accompanied by frequent cuffs, and blows, as the maddened Indians called him in the broken English which they had acquired, 'a tief, a hoss steal, a rascal,' which expressions the Indians had learned to intersperse with English oaths.

"In this condition of suffering Kenton remained through the day and through the night. The next morning the savages having collected their scattered horses, put Kenton upon a young colt, tied his hands behind him and his feet beneath the horse's belly, and set out on their return. The country was rough and Kenton could not at all protect himself from the brambles through which they passed. Thus they rode all day. When night came, their prisoner was bound to the earth as before. The next day they reached the Indian village, which was called Chilicothe, on the Miami River, forty or fifty miles west of the present city of Chilicothe, Ohio. A courier was sent forward, to inform the village of their arrival. Every man, woman and child came running out, to view the prisoner. One of their chiefs, Blackfish, approached Kenton with a strong hickory switch in his hand, and addressing him said,

"'You have been stealing our horses, have you?'

"'Yes,' was the defiant reply.

"'Did Colonel Boone,' inquired the chief, 'tell you to steal our horses?'

"'No,' said Kenton, 'I did it of my own accord.'

"Blackfish then with brawny arms so mercilessly applied the scourge to the bare head and shoulders of his prisoner, as to cause the blood to flow freely, and to occasion the acutest pain.

"In the meantime the whole crowd of men, women and children danced and hooted and clapped their hands, assailing him with the choicest epithets of Indian vituperation. With loud cries they demanded that he should be tied to the stake, that they might all enjoy the pleasure of tormenting him. A stake was immediately planted in the ground, and he was firmly fastened to it. His entire clothing was torn from him, mainly by the Indian women. The whole party then danced around him until midnight, yelling in the most frantic manner, smiting him with their hands and lacerating his flesh with their switches.

"At midnight they released him from the stake, and allowed him some little repose, in preparation for their principal amusement in the morning, of having their prisoner run the gauntlet. Three hundred Indians of all ages and both sexes were assembled for the savage festival. The Indians were ranged in two parallel lines, about six feet apart, all armed with sticks, hickory rods, whips, and other means of inflicting torture. Between these lines, for more than half a mile to the village, the wretched prisoner was doomed to run for his life, exposed to such injury as his tormentors could inflict as he passed. If he succeeded in reaching the council-house alive, it would prove an asylum to him for the present.

"At a given signal, Kenton started in the perilous race; exerting his utmost strength and activity, he passed swiftly along the line, receiving numerous blows, stripes, buffets, and wounds, until he approached the town, near which he saw an Indian leisurely awaiting his advance, with a drawn knife in his hand, intent upon his death.

"To avoid him, he instantly broke through the line, and made his rapid way towards the council-house, pursued by the promiscuous crowd, whooping and yelling like infernal furies at his heels. Entering the town in advance of his pursuers, just as he supposed the council-house within his reach, an Indian was perceived leisurely approaching him with his blanket wrapped around him; but suddenly he threw off the blanket and sprung upon Kenton as he advanced. Exhausted with fatigue and wounds, he was thrown to the ground, and in a moment he was beset with crowds, eager to inflict upon him the kick or blow which had been avoided by breaking through the line. Here beaten, kicked and scourged, until he was nearly lifeless, he was left to die."[2]

A few hours afterwards he was supplied with food and water, and was suffered to recuperate for a few days, until he was enabled to attend at the council-house, and receive the announcement of his final doom. It was here decided that he should be made a public sacrifice to the vengeance of the nation. The Indian town of Wappatomica, upon the present site of Zanesville, Ohio, was the appointed place of his execution. Being in a state of utter exhaustion his escape was deemed impossible, and he was carelessly guarded. In despair he attempted it. He was promptly recaptured and punished by being taken to a neighboring creek where he was dragged through mud and water, till life was nearly extinct. Still his constitutional vigor triumphed, and he revived.

Wappatomica was a British trading post. Here Kenton met an old comrade, Simon Girty, who had become a renegade, had joined the Indians, and had so adopted their dress and manners as hardly to be distinguished from his savage associates. Girty cautiously endeavored to save the condemned prisoner. He represented to the band that it would be of great advantage to them to have possession of one so intimately acquainted with all the white settlements and their resources.

---

[2] Macdonald's Sketches.

A respite was granted. Another council was held. The spirit of Indian revenge prevailed. Kenton was again doomed to death, to be preceded by the terrible ordeal of running the gauntlet.

But a British officer, influenced by the persuasions of the Indian chief Logan, the friend of the white man, urged upon the Indian chiefs that the British officers at Detroit would regard the possession of Kenton, with the information he had at his command, as a great acquisition, and that they would pay for him a ransom of at least one hundred dollars. They took him to Detroit; the ransom was paid, and Kenton became the prisoner of the British officers, instead of the savage chieftains. Still he was a prisoner, though treated with ordinary humanity, and was allowed the liberty of the town.

There were two other American captives there, Captain Nathan Bullit and Jesse Coffer. Escape seemed impossible, as it could only be effected through a wilderness four hundred miles in extent, crowded with wandering Indian bands, where they would be imminently exposed to recapture, or to death by starvation.

Simon Kenton was a very handsome man. He won the sympathies of a very kind English woman, Mrs. Harvey, the wife of one of the traders at the post. She secretly obtained for him and his two companions, and concealed in a hollow tree, powder, lead, moccasins, and a quantity of dried beef. One dark night, when the Indians were engaged in a drunken bout, she met Kenton in the garden and handed him three of the best rifles, which she had selected from those stacked near the house. The biographer of these events writes:

> "When a woman engages to do an action, she will risk limb, life or character, to serve him whom she respects or wishes to befriend. How differently the same action would be viewed by different persons! By Kenton and his friends her conduct was viewed as the benevolent conduct of a good angel; while if the part she played in behalf of Kenton and his companions had been known to the commander at Detroit, she would have been looked upon as a traitress, who merited the scorn and contempt of all honest citizens. This night was the last that Kenton ever saw or heard of her."

Our fugitives traveled mostly by night, guided by the stars. After passing through a series of wonderful adventures, which we have not space here to record, on the thirty-third day of their escape, they reached the settlement at the Falls of the Ohio, now Louisville. During the rest of the war, Kenton was a very active partisan. He died in the year 1836, over eighty years of age, having been for more than a quarter of a century an honored member of the Methodist Church.

Chapter 7

LIFE IN THE WILDERNESS

There were now four hungry men to occupy the little camp of our bold adventurers. They do not seem to have been conscious of enduring any hardships. The winter was mild. Their snug tent furnished perfect protection from wind and rain. With abundant fuel, their camp-fire ever blazed brightly. Still it was necessary for them to be diligent in hunting, to supply themselves with their daily food. Bread, eggs, milk, butter, sugar, and even salt, were articles of which they were entirely destitute.

One day, not long after the arrival of Squire Boone, Daniel Boone, with his companion Stewart, was a long distance from the camp, hunting. Suddenly the terrible war-whoop of the Indians resounded from a thicket, and a shower of arrows fell around them. Stewart, pierced by one of these deadly missiles, fell mortally wounded. A sturdy savage sprang from the ambuscade upon his victim, and with a yell buried a tomahawk in his brain. Then, grasping with one hand the hair on the top of his head, he made a rapid circular cut with his gleaming knife, and tore off the scalp, leaving the skull bare. The revolting deed was done quicker than it can be described. Shaking the bloody trophy in his hand, he gave a whoop of exultation which echoed far and wide through the solitudes of the forest.

Boone, swift of foot as the antelope, escaped and reached the camp with the sad tidings of the death of his companion, and of the presence, in their immediate vicinity, of hostile Indians. This so affrighted the North Carolinian who had come with Squire Boone, that he resolved upon an immediate return to the Yadkin. He set out alone, and doubtless perished by the way, as he was never heard of again. A skeleton, subsequently found in the wilderness, was supposed to be the remains of the unfortunate hunter. He probably perished through exhaustion, or by the arrow or tomahawk of the savage.

The two brothers, Daniel and Squire, were now left entirely alone.

They selected a favorable spot in a wild ravine where they would be the least likely to be discovered by hunting bands, and built for themselves a snug and comfortable log-house, in which they would be more effectually sheltered from the storms and cold of winter, and into which they moved from their open camp. Here they remained, two loving brothers of congenial tastes, during the months of January, February, March and April. Solitary as their life must have been probably, every hour brought busy employment. Each day's food was to be obtained by the rifle. Wood was to be procured for their fire. All their clothing, from the cap to the moccasin, was to be fashioned by their own hands from the skin of the deer, which they had carefully tanned into pliancy and softness; and there were to be added to their cabin many conveniences which required much ingenuity with knife and hatchet for their only tools, and with neither nail nor screw for their construction. In addition to this they were under the necessity of being ever on the alert to discover indications of the approach of the Indians.

The winter passed away, not only undisturbed, but evidently very happily. It is remarkable that their retreat was not discovered by any of the Indian bands, who in pursuit of game were constantly roving over those rich hunting grounds.

As summer's warmth returned, Squire Boone decided to retrace his steps to the Yadkin, to carry to his brother's family news of his safety, and to obtain much needed supplies of powder and of lead. There is no satisfactory explanation of the motives which could have induced Daniel, after the absence of a year from his home, to remain alone in that solitary cabin. In his autobiography he has assigned no reason for the extraordinary decision. One of the most judicious of his biographers makes the following statement which by no means solves the mystery:

"When the spring came it was time for another movement. The spring came early, and the awaking to its foliage seemed like the passing from night to the day. The game had reduced their powder and lead, and without these there was no existence to the white man. Again Daniel Boone rises to the emergency. It was necessary that the settlement which they had made should be continued and protected, and it was the duty in the progress of events that one of them should remain to that task. He made the selection and chose himself. He had the courage to remain alone. And while he felt the keenest desire to see his own family, he felt that he had a noble purpose to serve and was prepared for it."[3]

Daniel Boone, in his quaint autobiography, in the following terms alludes to the departure of his brother and his own solitary mode of life during the three months of his brother's absence:

"On the first day of May, 1770, my brother returned home to the settlement by himself for a new recruit of horses and ammunition, leaving me by myself without bread, salt or sugar, without company of my fellow creatures, or even a horse or dog. I confess I never before was under greater necessity of exercising philosophy and fortitude. A few days I passed uncomfortably. The idea of a beloved wife and family, and their anxiety on account of my absence and exposed situation, made sensible impressions on my heart. A thousand dreadful apprehensions presented themselves to my view, and had undoubtedly exposed me to melancholy if further indulged.
"One day I took a tour through the country, and the diversity and beauties of nature I met with in this charming season, expelled every gloomy and vexatious thought. Just at the close of the day the gentle gales retired and left the place to the disposal of a profound calm. Not a breeze shook the most tremulous leaf. I had gained the summit of a commanding ridge, and looking around with astonishing delight beheld the ample plain, the beauteous tracts below. On the other hand I surveyed

---

[3] Life of Boone, by W. H. Bogart.

the famous river Ohio, that rolled in silent dignity, marking the western boundary of Kentucky, with inconceivable grandeur. At a vast distance I beheld the mountains lift their venerable heads and penetrate the clouds.

"I kindled a fire near a fountain of sweet water, and feasted on the loin of a buck. The fallen shades of night soon overspread the whole hemisphere, and the earth seemed to gape after the hovering moisture. My roving excursion this day had fatigued my body and diverted my imagination. I laid me down to sleep, and I woke not until the sun had chased away the night. I continued this tour, and in a few days explored a considerable part of the country, each day equally pleased as the first. I returned to my old camp which was not disturbed in my absence. I did not confine my lodging to it, but often reposed in thick cane brakes, to avoid the savages, who I believe often visited it, but, fortunately for me, in my absence.

"In this situation I was constantly exposed to danger and death. How unhappy such a condition for a man tormented with fear, which is vain if no danger comes; and if it does, only augments the pain! It was my happiness to be destitute of this afflicting passion, with which I had the greatest reason to be affected. The prowling wolves diverted my nocturnal hours with perpetual howlings, and the various species of animals in this vast forest, in the day-time were continually in my view. Thus I was surrounded with plenty in the midst of want. I was happy in the midst of dangers and inconveniences. In such a diversity it was impossible I should be disposed to melancholy. No populous city, with all the varieties of commerce and stately structures, could afford so much pleasure to my mind, as the beauties of nature I found here.

"Thus through an uninterrupted scene of sylvan pleasures, I spent the time until the twenty-seventh day of July following, when my brother, to my great felicity, met me, according to appointment, at our old camp."

Boone was at this time thirty-six years of age. He was about five feet ten inches in height, and of remarkably vigorous and athletic frame. His life in the open air, his perfect temperance, and his freedom from all exciting passions, gave him constant health. Squire brought back to his brother the gratifying news that his wife Rebecca was in good health and spirits, and cheerfully acquiesced in whatever decision her husband might make, in reference to his absence. She had full confidence in the soundness of his judgment, and in his conjugal and parental love. The children were all well, and from the farm and the forest the wants of the family were fully supplied.

It appears that Squire Boone had succeeded in bringing one or two horses across the mountains. The abundance of grass kept them in fine condition. Upon the backs of these horses, the pioneers could traverse the treeless prairies without obstruction, and large portions of the forest were as free from underbrush as the park of an English nobleman. Invaluable as these animals were to the adventurers, they greatly increased their perils. They could not easily be concealed. Their footprints could not be effaced, and there was nothing the Indians coveted so greatly as a horse.

The two adventurers now set out on horseback for an exploring tour to the south-west. Following a line nearly parallel with the Cumberland Range, after traversing a magnificent region of beauty and fertility for about one hundred and fifty miles, they reached the banks of the Cumberland River. This majestic stream takes its rise on the western slope of the Cumberland Mountains. After an exceedingly circuitous route of six hundred miles, running far down into Tennessee, it turns north-westerly again, and empties its waters into the Ohio, about sixty miles above the entrance of that river into the Mississippi.

It was mid-summer. The weather was delightful. The forest free from underbrush, attractive as the most artificial park, and the smooth sweep of the treeless prairie presented before them as enticing a route of travel as the imagination could desire. There were of course hardships and privations, which would have been regarded as very severe by the dwellers in the sealed houses, but none which disturbed in the slightest degree the equanimity of these hardy adventurers. They journeyed very leisurely; seven months being occupied in the tour. Probably only a few miles were accomplished each day. With soft saddles made of the skin of buffalo, with their horses never urged beyond a walk, with bright skies above them, and vistas of beauty ever opening before them, and luxuriance, bloom and fragrance spread everywhere around, their journey seemed replete with enjoyment of the purest kind.

Though it was necessary to practice the extreme of caution, to avoid capture by the Indians, our adventurers do not seem to have been annoyed in the slightest degree with any painful fears on that account. Each morning they carefully scanned the horizon, to see if anywhere there could be seen the smoke of the camp-fire curling up from the open prairie or from the forest. Through the day they were ever on the alert, examining the trails which they occasionally passed, to see if there were any fresh foot prints, or other indications of the recent presence of their foe. At night, before venturing to kindle their own camp-fire, they looked cautiously in every direction, to see if a gleam from an Indian encampment could anywhere be seen. Thus from the first of August to the ensuing month of March, these two bold men traversed, for many hundred miles, an unknown country, filled with wandering hunting bands of hostile Indians, and yet avoided capture or detection.

If a storm arose, they would rear their cabin in some secluded dell, and basking in the warmth of their camp-fire wait until the returning sun invited them to resume their journey. Or if they came to some of nature's favored haunts, where Eden-like attractions were spread around them, on the borders of the lake, by the banks of the stream, or beneath the brow of the mountain, they would tarry for a few days, reveling in delights, which they both had the taste to appreciate.

In this way, they very thoroughly explored the upper valley of the Cumberland River. For some reason not given, they preferred to return north several hundred miles to the Kentucky River, as the seat of their contemplated settlement. The head waters of this stream are near those of the Cumberland. It however flows through the very heart of Kentucky, till it enters the Ohio River, midway between the present cities of Cincinnati and Louisville. It was in the month of March that they reached the Kentucky River on their return. For some time they wandered along its banks searching for the more suitable situation for the location of a colony.

"The exemption of these men," said W. H. Bogart, "from assault by the Indians during all this long period of seven months, in which, armed and on horseback, they seem to have roamed just where they chose, is most wonderful. It has something about it which seems like a special interposition of Providence, beyond the ordinary guardianship over the progress of man. On the safety of these men rested the hope of a nation. A very distinguished authority has declared, that without Boone, the settlements could not have been upheld and the conquest of Kentucky would have been reserved for the emigrants of the nineteenth century."

Boone having now, after an absence of nearly two years, apparently accomplished the great object of his mission; having, after the most careful and extensive exploration, selected such a spot as he deemed most attractive for the future home of his family, decided to return to the Yadkin and make preparations for their emigration across the mountains. To us now, such a movement seems to indicate an almost insane boldness and recklessness. To take wife and children into a pathless wilderness filled with unfriendly savages, five hundred miles from any of the settlements of civilization, would seem to invite death. A family could not long be concealed. Their discovery by the Indians would be almost the certain precursor of their destruction. Boone, in his autobiography, says in allusion to this hazardous adventure:

> "I returned home to my family with a determination to bring them as soon as possible, at the risk of my life and fortune, to live in Kentucky, which I esteemed a second paradise."

The two brothers accomplished the journey safely, and Daniel Boone found his family, after his long absence, in health and prosperity. One would have supposed that the charms of home on the banks of the Yadkin, where they could dwell in peace, abundance and safety, would have lured our adventurer to rest from his wanderings. And it is probable that for a time, he wavered in his resolution. Two years elapsed ere he set out for his new home in the Far-West.

There was much to be done in preparation for so momentous a movement. He sold his farm on the Yadkin and invested the proceeds in such comforts as would be available on the banks of the Kentucky. Money would be of no value to him there. A path had been discovered by which horses could be led through the mountains, and thus many articles could be transported which could not be taken in packs on the back. Several of the neighbors, elated by the description which Boone gave of the paradise he had found, were anxious to join his family in their emigration. There were also quite a number of young men rising here and there, who, lured by the romance of the adventure, were eager to accompany the expedition. All these events caused delays. The party of emigrants became more numerous than Boone at first expected.

It was not until the twenty-fifth of September, 1773, that Daniel Boone, his brother Squire, and quite a large party of emigrants, probably in all—men, women and children—not less than sixty in number, commenced their journey across the mountains. There were five families and forty pioneers, all well-armed, who were quite at home amid the trials and privations of the wilderness. Four horses, heavily laden, led the train through the narrow trails of the forest. Then came, in single file, the remainder of the party, of all ages and both sexes. It must have been a singular spectacle which was presented, as this long line wound its way through the valleys and over the ridges.

Squire Boone was quite familiar with the path. It was delightful autumnal weather. The days were long and calm, and yet not oppressively hot. There were no gloved gentlemen or delicate ladies in the company. All were hardy men and women, accustomed to endurance. Each day's journey was short. An hour before the sun disappeared in the west, the little village of cabins arose, where some spring gurgled from the cliff, or some sparkling mountain stream rippled before them. In front of each cabin the camp-fire blazed. All was animation and apparent joy, as the women prepared the evening meal, and the wearied children rested upon their couch of dried leaves or fragrant twigs. If a storm arose, they had but to remain beneath their shelter until it passed away.

"Traveling," says Madame de Stael, who was accustomed to the most luxurious of European conveyances, "is the most painful of pleasures." Probably our travelers on this journey experienced as many pleasures and as few pains as often fall to the lot of any tourist. The solitary wilderness has its attractions as well as the thronged town.

These bold men armed with their rifles, under such an accomplished leader as Daniel Boone, penetrated the wilderness with almost the strength of an invading army. Upon the open prairie, the superiority of their arms would compensate for almost any inferiority of numbers. Indeed they had little to fear from the savages, unless struck suddenly with overwhelming numbers leaping upon them from some ambush. Pleasant days came and went, while nothing occurred to interrupt the prosperity of their journey. They were approaching the celebrated Cumberland Gap, which seems to be a door that nature has thrown open for passing through this great mountain barrier. The vigilance they ought to have practiced had been in some degree relaxed by their freedom from all alarm. The cows had fallen a few miles behind, seven young men were with them, a son of Daniel Boone being one of the number. The main party was not aware how far the cattle had fallen in the rear.

It is probable that the savages had been following them for several days, watching for an opportunity to strike, for suddenly, as they were passing through a narrow ravine, the fearful war-whoop resounded from the thickets on both sides, a shower of arrows fell upon them, and six of the seven young men were instantly struck down by these deadly missiles. One only escaped. The attack was so sudden, so unexpected, that the emigrants had scarcely time for one discharge of their fire-arms, ere they were struck with death. The party in advance heard with consternation the reports of the muskets, and immediately returned to the scene of the disaster. But several miles intervened. They met the fugitive who had escaped, bleeding and almost breathless.

Hurrying on, an awful spectacle met their view. The bodies of six of the young men lay in the path, mangled and gory, with their scalps torn from their heads: the cattle were driven into the forest beyond pursuit. One of these victims was the eldest son of Daniel Boone. James was a noble lad of but seventeen years. His untimely death was a terrible blow to his father and mother. This massacre took place on the tenth of October, only a fortnight after the expedition had commenced its march. The gloom which it threw over the minds of the emigrants was so great, that the majority refused to press any farther into a wilderness where they would encounter such perils.

They had already passed two mountain ridges. Between them there was a very beautiful valley, through which flows the Clinch River. This many leagues below, uniting with the Holston River, flowing on the other side of Powell's Ridge, composes the majestic Tennessee, which, extending far down into Alabama, turns again north, and traversing the whole breadth of Tennessee and Kentucky, empties into the Ohio.

Notwithstanding the remonstrances of Daniel Boone and his brother, the majority of the emigrants resolved to retreat forty miles over the Walden Ridge, and establish themselves in the valley of the Clinch. Daniel Boone, finding all his attempts to encourage them to proceed in vain, decided with his customary good sense to acquiesce in their wishes, and quietly to await further developments. The whole party consequently retraced their steps, and reared their cabins on fertile meadows in the valley of the Clinch River. Here, between parallel ridges of mountains running north-east and south-west, Boone with his disheartened emigrants passed seven months. This settlement was within the limits of the present State of Virginia, in its most extreme south-western corner.

The value of the vast country beyond the mountains was beginning to attract the attention of the governors of the several colonies. Governor Dunmore of Virginia had sent a party of surveyors to explore the valley of the Ohio River as far as the celebrated Falls of the Ohio, near the present site of Louisville. Quite a body of these surveyors had built and fortified a camp near the Falls, and were busy in exploring the country, in preparation for the granting of lands as rewards for services to the officers and soldiers in the French war. These pioneers were far away in the wilderness, four hundred miles beyond any settlement of the whites. They were surrounded by thousands of Indian warriors, and still they felt somewhat secure, as a treaty of peace had been made by the Governor of Virginia with the neighboring chiefs. But, notwithstanding this treaty, many of the more intelligent of the Indians foresaw the inevitable destruction of their hunting grounds, should the white men succeed in establishing themselves on their lands, and cutting them up into farms.

A friendly Indian had informed Governor Dunmore that a very formidable conspiracy had been organised by the tribes for the destruction of the party encamped at the Falls of the Ohio, and for the extermination of every other party of whites who should penetrate their hunting grounds. It was in accordance with this conspiracy that Daniel Boone's party was so fiercely assailed when near the Gap, in the Cumberland Mountains; and it was probably the knowledge of this conspiracy, thus practically developed, which led the husbands and fathers to abandon their enterprise of plunging into the wilderness of Kentucky.

There were about forty men all numbered, in the little band of surveyors at the Falls. They were in terrible peril. Unconscious of danger, and supposing the Indians to be friendly, they were liable to be attacked on any day by overwhelming numbers of savages, and utterly exterminated. It consequently became a matter of great moment that Governor Dunmore should send them word of their danger, and if possible secure their safe return to the settlements. But who would undertake such a mission? One fraught with greater danger could not easily be imagined. The courier must traverse on foot a distance of four or five hundred miles through a pathless wilderness, filled with hunting bands of hostile savages. He must live upon the game he could shoot each day, when every discharge of his musket was liable to bring upon him scores of foes. He must either eat his food raw, or cook it at a fire whose gleam at night, or smoke by day, would be almost sure to attract the attention of death-dealing enemies. He must conceal his footprints from hunting bands, wandering far and wide in every direction, so keen in their sagacity that they could almost follow the track of the lightest-footed animal through the forest or over the prairie.

The Indians had also well-trained dogs, who being once put upon the scent, could with unerring instinct follow any object of search, until it was overtaken.

The name of Daniel Boone was mentioned to Governor Dunmore as precisely the man to meet this exigency. The Governor made application to the practiced hunter, and Boone, without the slightest hesitancy, accepted the perilous office. Indeed he seems to have been entirely unconscious of the heroism he was developing. Never did knight errant of the middle ages undertake an achievement of equal daring; for capture not only was certain death, but death under the most frightful tortures. But Boone, calm, imperturbable, pensive, with never a shade of boastfulness in word or action, embarked in the enterprise as if it had been merely one of the ordinary occurrences of every-day life. In the following modest words he records the event in his autobiography:

> "I remained with my family on the Clinch river until the sixth of June, 1774, when I, and one Michael Stoner, were solicited by Governor Dunmore of Virginia, to go to the Falls of the Ohio to conduct into the settlements a number of surveyors that had been sent thither by him some months before, this country having about this time drawn the attention of many adventurers. We immediately complied with the Governor's request, and conducted in the surveyors, completing a tour of eight hundred miles, through many difficulties, in sixty-two days."

The narrative which follows will give the reader some idea of the wilderness which Boone was about to penetrate and the perils which he was to encounter.

An emigrant of these early days who lived to witness the transformation of the wilderness from a scene of unbroken solitude into the haunts of busy men, in the following words describes this change and its influence upon the mind:

> "To a person who has witnessed all the changes which have taken place in the western country since its first settlement, its former appearance is like a dream or romance. He will find it difficult to realise the features of that wilderness which was the abode of his infant days. The little cabin of his father no longer exists. The little field and truck patch which gave him a scanty supply of coarse bread and vegetables have been swallowed up in the extended meadows, orchard or grain fields. The rude fort in which his people had resided so many painful summers has vanished.
>
> "Everywhere surrounded by the busy hum of men and the splendor, arts, refinements and comforts of civilised life, his former state and that of his country have vanished from his memory; or if sometimes he

bestows a reflection on its original aspect, the mind seems to be carried back to a period of time much more remote than it really is. One advantage at least results from having lived in a state of society ever on the change and always for the better, that it doubles the retrospect of life. With me at any rate it has had that effect. Did not the definite number of my years teach me to the contrary, I should think myself at least one hundred years old instead of fifty. The case is said to be widely different with those who have passed their lives in cities or ancient settlements where, from year to year, the same unchanging aspect of things presents itself.

"One prominent feature of the wilderness is its solitude. Those who plunged into the bosom of this forest left behind them not only the busy hum of men, but of domesticated animal life generally. The solitude of the night was interrupted only by the howl of the wolf, the melancholy moan of the ill-boding owl or the shriek of the frightful panther. Even the faithful dog, the only steadfast companion of man among the brute creation, partook of the silence of the desert; the discipline of his master forbade him to bark or move but in obedience to his command, and his native sagacity soon taught the propriety of obedience to this severe government.

"The day was, if possible, more solitary than the night. The noise of the wild turkey, the croaking of the raven, or the woodpecker tapping the hollow beech tree, did not much enliven the dreary scene. The various tribes of singing birds are not inhabitants of the desert. They are not carnivorous and therefore must be fed from the labors of man. At any rate they did not exist in this country at its first settlement.

"Let the imagination of the reader pursue the track of the adventurer into the solitary wilderness, bending his course towards the setting sun over undulating hills, under the shade of large forest trees, and wading through the rank weeds and grass which then covered the earth. Now he views from the top of a hill the winding course of a creek whose streams he wishes to explore. Doubtful of its course and of his own, he ascertains the cardinal points of north and south by the thickness of the moss and bark on the north side of the ancient trees. Now descending into a valley, he presages his approach to a river by seeing large ash, basswood and sugar trees beautifully festooned with wild grape vines. Watchful as Argus, his restless eye catches everything around him.

"In an unknown region and surrounded with dangers, he is the sentinel of his own safety and relies on himself for protection. The toilsome march of the day being ended, at the fall of night he seeks for safety some narrow sequestered hollow, and by the side of a large log builds a fire and, after eating a coarse and scanty meal, wraps himself up in his blanket and lays himself down for repose on his bed of leaves, with his feet to the fire, hoping for favorable dreams, ominous of future good luck, while his faithful dog and gun rest by his side.

"But let not the reader suppose that the pilgrim of the wilderness could feast his imagination with the romantic beauties of nature, without any drawback from conflicting passions. His situation did not afford him much time for contemplation. He was an exile from the warm clothing and plentiful mansions of society. His homely woodman's dress soon became old and ragged. The cravings of hunger compelled him to sustain from day to day the fatigues of the chase. Often he had to eat his venison, bear's meat, or wild turkey without bread or salt. His situation was not without its dangers. He did not know at what moment his foot might be stung by a serpent, at what moment he might meet with the formidable bear, or on what limb of a tree over his head the murderous panther might be perched, in a squatting attitude, to drop down upon him and tear him in pieces in a moment.

"Exiled from society and its comforts, the situation of the first adventurers was perilous in the extreme. The bite of a serpent, a broken limb, a wound of any kind, or a fit of sickness in the wilderness without those accommodations which wounds and sickness require, was a dreadful calamity. The bed of sickness, without medical aid, and above all to be destitute of the kind attention of a mother, sister, wife, or other female friends, was a situation which could not be anticipated by the tenant of the forest, with other sentiments than those of the deepest horror."[4]

There are no narratives of more thrilling interest than those which describe the perils and hair-breadth escapes which some of these bold hunters encountered. Immediately after the purchase of Louisiana, an expedition under Lewis and Clark was fitted out, under President

---

[4] Doddridge's Notes.

Jefferson's administration, to explore the vast, mysterious, undefined realms which the government had purchased. In the month of May, 1804, the expedition, in birch canoes, commenced the ascent of the Missouri river.

They knew not whence its source, what its length or the number of its tributaries, through what regions of fertility or barrenness it flowed, or what the character of the nations who might inhabit its banks. Paddling up the rapid current of this flood of waters in their frail boats, the ascent was slow. By the latter part of October they had reached a point fifteen hundred miles above the spot where the Missouri enters the Mississippi. Here they spent the winter with some friendly Indians called the Mandans.

Early in April, Lewis and Clark, with thirty men in their canoes, resumed their voyage. Their course was nearly west. In May they reached the mouth of the Yellow Stone River, and on the 13th of June came to the *Great Falls of the Missouri*. Here they found a series of cataracts ten miles in length. At one spot the river plunged over a precipice eighty-seven feet in height. Carrying their canoes around these falls, they re-embarked, and paddled through what they called "The Gates of the Rocky Mountains." Here for six miles they were in a narrow channel with perpendicular walls of rock, rising on both sides to the height of twelve hundred feet. Thus these adventurers continued their voyage till they reached the head of navigation, three thousand miles from the mouth of the Missouri river. Passing through the mountains they launched their canoes on streams flowing to the west, through which they entered the Columbia River, reaching its mouth, through a thousand perils on the 15th of November. They were now more than four thousand miles distant from the mouth of the Missouri. Such was the breadth of the estate we had purchased of France.

Here they passed their second winter. In the early spring they commenced their return. When they arrived at the Falls of the Missouri they encountered a numerous band of Indians, very bold and daring, called the Blackfoot. These savages were astonished beyond measure, at the effect of the rifle which could emit thunder and lightning, and a deadly though invisible bolt. Some of the boldest endeavored to wrench the rifles from some of the Americans. Mr. Lewis found it necessary to shoot one of them before they would desist. The rest fled in dismay, but burning with the desire for revenge. The explorers continuing their voyage arrived at Saint Louis on the 23rd of September, 1806, having been absent more than two years, and having traveled more than nine thousand miles.

When the expedition, on its return, had reached the head waters of the Missouri, two of these fearless men, Colter and Potts, decided to remain in the wilderness to hunt beaver. Being well aware of the hostility of the Blackfoot Indians, within whose regions they were, they set their traps at night, and took them up in the first dawn of the day. Early one morning, they were ascending a creek in a canoe, visiting their traps, when they were alarmed by a great noise, like the trampling of animals. They could see nothing, as the perpendicular banks of the river impeded their view. Yet they hoped that the noise was occasioned simply by the rush of a herd of buffaloes.

Their doubts were soon painfully removed. A band of six hundred Blackfoot warriors appeared upon each side of the creek. Escape was hopeless. The Indians beckoned to the hunters to come ashore. Colter turned the head of the canoe towards the bank, and as soon as it touched the land, a burly savage seized the rifle belonging to Potts, and wrenched it from his hand. But Colter, who was a man of extraordinary activity and strength, grasped the rifle, tore it from the hands of the Indian, and handed it back to Potts. Colter stepped ashore and was a captive. Potts, with apparent infatuation, but probably influenced by deliberate thought, pushed again out into the stream. He knew that, as a captive, death by horrible torture awaited him. He preferred to provoke the savages to his instant destruction. An arrow was shot at him, which pierced his body. He took deliberate aim at the Indian who threw it and shot him dead upon the spot. Instantly a shower of arrows whizzed through the air, and he fell a dead man in the bottom of the boat. The earthly troubles of Potts were ended. But fearful were those upon which Colter was about to enter.

The Indians, after some deliberation respecting the manner in which they would put him to death, stripped him entirely naked, and one of the chiefs led him out upon the prairie to the distance of three or four hundred yards from the rest of the band who were grouped together. Colter then perceived that he was to have the dreadful privilege of running for his life;—he, entirely naked and unarmed, to be pursued by six hundred fleet-footed Indians with arrows and javelins, and with their feet and limbs protected from thorns and brambles by moccasins and deerskin leggins.

"Save yourself if you can," said the chief in the Blackfoot language as he set him loose. Colter sprung forward with almost supernatural speed. Instantly the Indian's war-whoop burst from the lips of his six hundred pursuers. They were upon a plain about six miles in breadth abounding with the prickly pear. At the end of the plain there was Jefferson River, a stream but a few rods wide. Every step Colter took, bounding forward with almost the speed of an antelope, his naked feet were torn by the thorns. The physical effort he made was so great that the blood gushed from his nostrils, and flowed profusely down over his chest. He had half crossed the plain before he ventured to glance over his shoulder upon his pursuers, who, with hideous yells, like baying bloodhounds, seemed close upon his heels. Much to his relief he perceived that he had greatly distanced most of the Indians, though one stout savage, with a javelin in his hand, was within a hundred yards of him.

Hope reanimated him. Regardless of lacerated feet and blood, he pressed forward with renovated vigor until he arrived within about a mile of the river, when he found that his pursuer was gaining rapidly upon him. He could hear his breathing and the sound of his footsteps, and expected every moment to feel the sharp javelin piercing his back.

In his desperation he suddenly stopped, turned round and stretching out both of his arms, rushed, in his utter defencelessness, upon the armed warrior. The savage, startled by this unexpected movement and by the bloody appearance of his victim, stumbled and fell, breaking his spear as he attempted to throw it. Colter instantly snatched up the pointed part, and pinned his foe, quivering with convulsions to the earth.

Again he plunged forward on the race for life. The Indians, as they came up, stopped for a moment around the body of their slain comrade, and then, with hideous yells, resumed the pursuit. The stream was fringed with a dense growth of cotton-wood trees. Colter rushed through them, thus concealed from observation, and seeing near by a large raft of drift timber, he plunged into the water, dived under the raft and fortunately succeeded in getting his head above the water between the logs, where smaller wood covered him to the depth of several feet.

Scarcely had he attained this hiding place ere the Indians like so many fiends came rushing down to the river's bank. They searched the cottonwood thickets, and traversed the raft in all directions. They frequently came so near the hiding place of Colter that he could see them through the chinks. He was terribly afraid that they would set fire to the raft. Night came on, and the Indians disappeared. Colter, in the darkness, dived from under the raft, swam down the river to a considerable distance, and then landed and traveled all night, following the course of the stream.

"Although happy in having escaped from the Indians, his situation was still dreadful. He was completely naked under a burning sun. The soles of his feet were filled with the thorns of the prickly pear. He was hungry and had no means of killing game, although he saw abundance around him; and was at a great distance from the nearest settlement. After some days of sore travel, during which he had no other sustenance than the root known by naturalists under the name of *psoralea esculenta*, he at length arrived in safety at Lisa Fort, on the Big Horn, a branch of the Yellow Stone River."

Chapter 8

CAPTIVITY AND FLIGHT

The following well authenticated account of the adventures of a ranger is so graphically described in Brown's *History of Illinois*, that we give it in the words of the writer:

"Thomas Higgins, a native Kentuckian, was, in the summer of 1814, stationed in a block-house eight miles south of Greenville, in what is now Bond County, Illinois. On the evening of the 30th of August, 1814, a small party of Indians having been seen prowling about the station, Lieutenant Journay, with all his men, twelve only in number, sallied forth the next morning, just before daybreak, in pursuit of them. They had not proceeded far on the border of the prairie, before they were in an ambuscade of seventy or eighty savages. At the first fire, the lieutenant and three of his men were killed. Six fled to the fort under cover of the smoke, for the morning was sultry, and the air being damp, the smoke from the guns hung like a cloud over the scene. But Higgins remained behind to have 'one more pull at the enemy,' and to avenge the death of his companions.

"He sprang behind a small elm scarcely sufficient to protect his body, when, the smoke partly rising, discovered to him a number of Indians, upon whom he fired, and shot down the foremost one. Concealed still by the smoke, Higgins reloaded, mounted his horse, and turned to fly, when a voice, apparently from the grass, hailed him with: Tom, you won't leave me, will you?

"He turned immediately around, and seeing a fellow soldier by the name of Burgess lying on the ground, wounded and gasping for breath, replied, 'No, I will not leave you; come along.' 'I can't come,' said Burgess, 'my leg is all smashed to pieces.'

"Higgins dismounted, and taking up his friend, whose ankle had been broken, was about to lift him on his horse, when the animal, taking fright, darted off in an instant and left them both behind. 'This is too bad,' said Higgins, 'but don't fear. You hop off on your three legs and I will stay behind between you and the Indians and keep them off. Get into the tallest grass and creep as near the ground as possible.' Burgess did so and escaped.

"The smoke which had hitherto concealed Higgins now cleared away, and he resolved, if possible, to retreat. To follow the track of Burgess was most expedient. It would, however, endanger his friend. He determined, therefore, to venture boldly forward and, if discovered, to secure his own safety by the rapidity of his flight. On leaving a small thicket in which he had sought refuge, he discovered a tall, portly savage nearby, and two others in the direction between him and the fort.

"He started, therefore, for a little rivulet near, but found one of his limbs failing him, it having been struck by a ball in the first encounter, of which, till now, he was scarcely conscious. The largest Indian pressed close upon him, and Higgins turned round two or three times in order to fire. The Indian halted and danced about to prevent his taking aim. He saw that it was unsafe to fire at random, and perceiving two others approaching, knew that he must be overpowered unless he could dispose of the forward Indian first. He resolved, therefore, to halt and receive his fire.

"The Indian raised his rifle, and Higgins, watching his eye, turned suddenly as his finger pressed the trigger, and received the ball in his thigh. He fell, but rose immediately and ran. The foremost Indian, now certain of his prey, loaded again, and with the other two pressed on. They overtook him. He fell again, and as he rose the whole three fired, and he received all their balls. He now fell and rose a third time, and the Indians, throwing away their guns, advanced upon him with spears and knives. As he presented his gun at one or another, each fell back. At last the largest

Indian, supposing his gun to be empty, from his fire having been thus reserved, advanced boldly to the charge. Higgins fired and the savage fell.

"He had now four bullets in his body, an empty gun in his hand, two Indians unharmed as yet before him, and a whole tribe but a few yards distant. Any other man would have despaired. Not so with him. He had slain the most dangerous of the three, and having but little to fear from the others, began to load his rifle. They raised a savage whoop and rushed to the encounter. A bloody conflict now ensued. The Indians stabbed him in several places. Their spears, however, were but thin poles, hastily prepared, and which bent whenever they struck a rib or a muscle. The wounds they made were not therefore deep, though numerous.

"At last one of them threw his tomahawk. It struck him upon the cheek, severed his ear, laid bare his skull to the back of his head, and stretched him upon the prairie. The Indians again rushed on, but Higgins, recovering his self-possession, kept them off with his feet and hands. Grasping at length one of their spears, the Indian, in attempting to pull it from him, raised Higgins up, who, taking his rifle, dashed out the brains of the nearest savage. In doing this, however, it broke, the barrel only remaining in his hand. The other Indian, who had heretofore fought with caution, came now manfully into the battle. His character as a warrior was in jeopardy. To have fled from a man thus wounded and disarmed, or to have suffered his victim to escape, would have tarnished his fame forever. Uttering, therefore, a terrific yell, he rushed on and attempted to stab the exhausted ranger. But the latter warded off his blow with one hand and brandished his rifle barrel with the other. The Indian was as yet unharmed, and, under existing circumstances, by far the most powerful man. Higgins' courage, however, was unexhausted and inexhaustible.

"The savage at last began to retreat from the glare of his untamed eye to the spot where he had dropped his rifle. Higgins knew that if he recovered that, his own case was desperate. Throwing, therefore, his rifle barrel aside, and drawing his hunting knife he rushed upon his foe. A desperate strife ensued—deep gashes were inflicted on both sides. Higgins, fatigued and exhausted by the loss of blood, was no longer a match for the savage. The latter succeeded in throwing his adversary from him, and went immediately in pursuit of his rifle. Higgins at the same time rose and sought for the gun of the other Indian. Both, therefore, bleeding and out of breath, were in search of arms to renew the combat.

"The smoke had now passed away, and a large number of Indians were in view. Nothing, it would seem, could now save the gallant ranger. There was, however, an eye to pity and an arm to save, and that arm was a woman's. The little garrison had witnessed the whole combat. It consisted of but six men and one woman; that woman, however, was a host—a Mrs. Pursley. When she saw Higgins contending single-handed with a whole tribe of savages, she urged the rangers to attempt his rescue. The rangers objected, as the Indians were ten to one. Mrs. Pursley, therefore, snatched a rifle from her husband's hand, and declaring that 'so fine a fellow as Tom Higgins should not be lost for want of help,' mounted a horse and sallied forth to his rescue.

"The men, unwilling to be outdone by a woman, followed at full gallop, reached the spot where Higgins had fainted and fell, before the Indians came up, and while the savage with whom he had been engaged was looking for his rifle, his friends lifted the wounded ranger up and throwing him across a horse before one of the party, reached the fort in safety.

"Higgins was insensible for several days, and his life was preserved by continued care. His friends extracted two of the balls from his thigh. Two, however, yet remained, one of which gave him a good deal of pain. Hearing afterwards that a physician had settled within a day's ride of him, he determined to go and see him. The physician asked him fifty dollars for the operation. This Higgins flatly refused, saying that it was more than half a year's pension. On reaching home he found that the exercise of riding had made the ball discernable; he requested his wife, therefore, to hand him his razor. With her assistance he laid open his thigh until the edge of the razor touched the bullet, then, inserting his two thumbs into the gash, 'he flirted it out,' as he used to say, 'without it costing him a cent.'

"The other ball yet remained. It gave him, however, but little pain, and he carried it with him to the grave. Higgins died in Fayette County, Illinois, a few years ago. He was the most perfect specimen of a frontier man in his day, and was once assistant door-keeper of the House of Representatives in Illinois. The facts above stated are familiar to many to whom Higgins was personally known, and there is no doubt of their correctness."[5]

This narrative gives one a very vivid idea of the nature of the conflict in which Boone, through so many years of his life, was engaged. The little fort, whose feeble garrison he commanded, was liable at any time to be assailed by overwhelming numbers.

Daniel Boone, during his occupancy of the fort at Boonesborough, manifested the most constant vigilance to guard against surprise. He was however struggling against a foe whose cunning and strategems were such, as not to allow him an hour of quiet. One morning two men laboring in the field were shot at by the Indians. Not being hit, they ran for the fort. They were pursued by the savages, and one was tomahawked and scalped within a few hundred feet of the gate. Boone hearing the alarm, inconsiderately rushed out with ten men upon the miscreants. They fled before him hotly pursued. In the eagerness of the chase, Boone had not counted the number of his foes. Some of them rushing from their ambush cut off his retreat. At one discharge, six of his men fell wounded. Boone's leg was shattered by a ball.

As he fell to the ground, the tomahawk of a savage was over his head. Simon Kenton, who was one of Boone's party, with sure aim pierced the heart of the savage with a rifle bullet and he fell dead. Reinforcements rushed from the fort, and fortunately succeeded in rescuing the adventurous party, the wounded and all. It is said of Boone, that though a silent man and not given to compliments, he manifested very deep gratitude to his friend Kenton for saving his life. The very peculiar character of Boone is vividly presented in the following sketch, from the graphic pen of Mr. Peck:

"As dangers thickened and appearances grew more alarming, as scouts came in with rumors of Indians seen here and there, and as the hardy and bold woodsmen sat around their camp-fires with the loaded rifle at hand, rehearsing for the twentieth time the tales of noble daring, or

---

[5] Brown's Illinois.

the hair-breadth escapes, Boone would sit silent, apparently not heeding the conversation, employed in repairing the rents in his hunting shirt and leggins, moulding bullets or cleaning his rifle. Yet the eyes of the garrison were upon him. Concerning 'Indian signs' he was an oracle.

"Sometimes with one or two trusty companions, but more frequently alone, as night closed in, he would steal noiselessly away into the woods, to reconnoiter the surrounding wilderness. And in the day time, stealthily would he creep along with his trusty rifle resting on his arm, ready for the least sign of danger, his keen, piercing eyes glancing into every thicket and canebrake, or watch intently for 'signs' of the wiley enemy. Accustomed to range the country as a hunter and a scout, he would frequently meet the approaching travelers on the road and pilot them into the settlement, while his rifle supplied them with provisions. He was ever more ready to aid the community, or to engage in public services, than to attend to his private interests."

The want of salt had become one of the greatest privations of the garrison. It was an article essential to comfort and health, and yet, in the warfare then existing, was almost impossible of attainment. Upon the Sicking River, nearly a hundred miles north from Boonesborough, there were valuable springs richly impregnated with salt. Animals from all quarters frequented these springs, licking the saturated clay around them. Hence the name of Salt Licks. Evaporating the water by boiling in large kettles, salt of a good quality was easily obtained. The necessities of the garrison became so great, that Colonel Boone took a well-armed party of thirty men, and threading their way through the wilderness, at length reached the springs unassailed. It was one of the boldest of adventures. It was certain that the watchful Indians would learn that a party had left the cover of the fort, and would fall upon them with great ferocity.

Colonel Boone, who desired to obtain salt for all the garrisons, deemed it consequently necessary to work night and day with the greatest possible diligence. They could never venture to move a step beyond the grasp of their rifles. For nearly four weeks the salt-makers pursued their work unassailed. The news of so strong and well-armed a party having left the fort, reached the ears of the Indians. They had a very great dread of Boone,

Captivity and Flight

and knew very well he would not be found sleeping or unprotected, at the springs. They shrewdly inferred that the departure of so many men must greatly weaken the garrison, and that they could never hope for a more favorable opportunity to attack Boonesborough.

This formidable fortress was the great object of their dread. They thought that if they could lay it in ashes, making it the funeral pyre of all its inmates, the weaker forts would be immediately abandoned by their garrisons in despair, or could easily be captured. An expedition was formed, consisting of more than a hundred Indian warriors, and accompanied it is said by two Frenchmen. Boone had sent three men back to the garrison, loaded with salt, and to convey tidings of the good condition of the party at the springs.

On the morning of the seventh of February, Boone, who was unequalled in his skill as a hunter, and also in the sagacity by which he could avoid the Indians, was out in search of game as food for the party. Emboldened by the absence of all signs of the vicinity of the Indians, he had wandered some distance from the springs, where he encountered this band of warriors, attended by the two Frenchmen, on the march for the assault on Boonesborough. Though exceedingly fleet of foot, his attempt to escape was in vain. The young Indian runners overtook and captured him.

The Indians seem to have had great respect for Boone. Even with them he had acquired the reputation of being a just and humane man, while his extraordinary abilities, both as a hunter and a warrior, had won their admiration. Boone was not heading a war party to assail them. He had not robbed them of any of their horses. They were therefore not exasperated against him personally. It is also not improbable that the Frenchmen who were with them had influenced them not to treat their prisoner with barbarity.

Boone, whose spirits seemed never to be perturbed, yielded so gracefully to his captors as to awaken in their bosoms some emotions of kindness. They promised that if the party at the springs would yield without resistance—which resistance, though unavailing, they knew would cost them the lives of many of their warriors—the lives of the captives should be safe, and they should not be exposed to any inhuman treatment.

Boone was much perplexed. Had he been with his men, he would have fought to the last extremity, and his presence not improbably might have inspirited them, even to a successful defence. But deprived of their leader, taken entirely by surprise, and outnumbered three or four to one, their massacre was certain. And it was also certain that the Indians, exasperated by the loss which they would have encountered, would put every prisoner to death, through all the horrors of fiendlike torture.

Under these circumstances, Colonel Boone very wisely decided upon surrender. It would have been very impolitic and cruel to do otherwise. He having thus given his word, the Indians placed implicit confidence in it. They were also perfectly faithful to their own promises. Boone was allowed to approach his men, and represent the necessity of a surrender, which was immediately effected. The Indians were so elated by this great victory, and were so well satisfied with the result of the campaign, that instead of continuing their march for the attack of Boonesborough, they returned with their illustrious captive and his twenty-seven companions to their head-quarters on the Little Miami River.

The modest, unaffected account which Boone himself gives of these transactions, is worthy of record here:

> "On the seventh of February, as I was hunting to procure meat for the company, I met a party of one hundred and two Indians, and two Frenchmen, on their march against Boonesborough; that place being particularly the object of the enemy. They pursued and took me, and brought me the eighth day to the Licks, where twenty-seven of my party were, three of them having previously returned home with the salt. I, knowing it was impossible for them to escape, capitulated with the enemy, and at a distance, in their view, gave notice to my men of their situation with orders not to resist, but surrender themselves captives.
>
> "The generous usage the Indians had promised before in my capitulation, was afterwards fully complied with, and we proceeded with them as prisoners to Old Chilicothe, the principal Indian town on Little Miami, where we arrived, after an uncomfortable journey in very severe weather, on the eighteenth of February, and received as good treatment as prisoners could expect from savages. On the tenth of March following, I

and ten of my men were conducted by forty Indians to Detroit, where we arrived the thirtieth day, and were treated by Governor Hamilton, the British commander at that post, with great humanity.

"During our travels, the Indians entertained me well, and their affection for me was so great, that they utterly refused to leave me there with the others, although the Governor offered them one hundred pounds sterling for me, on purpose to give me a parole to go home. Several English gentlemen there, being sensible of my adverse fortune, and touched with human sympathy, generously offered a friendly supply for my wants, which I refused with many thanks for their kindness, adding that I never expected it would be in my power to recompense such unmerited generosity."

The British officers in Detroit could not venture to interfere in behalf of Colonel Boone, in any way which would displease their savage allies, for they relied much upon them in their warfare against the colonies.

There was much in the character of our hero to win the affection of the savages. His silent, unboastful courage they admired. He was more than their equal in his skill in traversing the pathless forest. His prowess as a hunter they fully appreciated. It was their hope that he would consent to be incorporated in their tribe, and they would gladly have accepted him as one of their chiefs. The savages had almost universally sufficient intelligence to appreciate the vast superiority of the white man.

The Indians spent ten days at Detroit, and surrendered, for a ransom, all their captives to the English, excepting Colonel Boone. Him they took back on a long and fatiguing journey to Old Chilicothe on the Little Miami. The country they traversed, now so full of wealth, activity, and all the resources of individual and social happiness, was then a vast wilderness, silent and lonely. Still in its solitude it was very beautiful, embellished with fertile plains, magnificent groves, and crystal streams. At Chilicothe, Colonel Boone was formally adopted, according to an Indian custom, into the family of Blackfish, one of the distinguished chiefs of the Shawanese tribe.

"At Chilicothe," writes Boone, "I spent my time as comfortably as I could expect. I was adopted according to their custom, into a family where

I became a son, and had a great share in the affection of my new parents, brothers, sisters and friends. I was exceedingly familiar and friendly with them, always appearing as cheerful and satisfied as possible, and they put great confidence in me. I often went hunting with them, and frequently gained their applause for my activity, at our shooting matches. I was careful not to excel them when shooting, for no people are more envious than they in their sport. I could observe in their countenances and gestures, the greatest expressions of joy when they exceeded me, and when the reverse happened, of envy. The Shawanese king took great notice of me, and treated me with profound respect and entire friendship, often trusting me to hunt at my liberty. I frequently returned with the spoils of the woods, and as often presented some of what I had taken to him, expressive of my duty to my sovereign. My food and lodging were in common with them. Not so good, indeed, as I could desire, but necessity makes everything acceptable."

The spirit manifested by Boone under these circumstances, when he was apparently a hopeless prisoner in the hands of the Indians, was not influenced by artifice alone. He had real sympathy for the savages, being fully conscious of the wrongs which were often inflicted upon them, and which goaded their untamed natures to fearful barbarities. He had always treated them not only kindly, but with fraternal respect. The generous treatment he had received in return won his regards. His peculiarly placid nature was not easily disturbed by any reverses. Let what would happen, he never allowed himself to complain or to worry. Thus making the best of circumstances, he always looked upon the brightest side of things, and was reasonably happy, even in this direful captivity. Still he could not forget his home, and was continually on the alert to avail himself of whatever opportunity might be presented to escape and return to his friends.

The ceremony of adoption was pretty severe and painful. All the hair of the head was plucked out by a tedious operation, leaving simply a tuft three or four inches in diameter on the crown. This was called the scalp-lock. The hair was here allowed to grow long, and was dressed with ribbons and feathers. It was to an individual warrior what the banner is to an army. The victor tore it from the skull as his trophy. Having thus denuded the head and dressed the scalp-lock, the candidate was taken to the river and very thoroughly scrubbed, that all the white blood might be washed out of him. His face was painted in the most approved style of Indian taste, when he was led to the council lodge and addressed by the chief in a long and formal speech, in which he expatiates upon the honor conferred upon the adopted son, and upon the corresponding duties expected of him.

Colonel Boone having passed through this transformation, with his Indian dress and his painted cheeks, his tufted scalp-lock and his whole person embrowned by constant exposure to the open air, could scarcely be distinguished from any of his Indian associates. His wary captors however, notwithstanding all the kindness with which they treated him, seemed to be conscious that it must be his desire to return to his friends. They therefore habitually, but without a remark suggestive of any suspicions, adopted precautions to prevent his escape. So skilful a hunter as Boone could, with his rifle and a supply of ammunition, traverse the solitary expanse around for almost any length of time, living in abundance. But deprived of his rifle or of ammunition, he would soon almost inevitably perish of starvation. The Indians were therefore very careful not to allow him to accumulate any ammunition, which was so essential to sustain him in a journey through the wilderness.

Though Boone was often allowed to go out alone to hunt, they always counted his balls and the charges of powder. Thus they could judge whether he had concealed any ammunition to aid him, should he attempt to escape. He however, with equal sagacity, cut the balls in halves, and used very small charges of powder. Thus he secretly laid aside quite a little store of ammunition. As ever undismayed by misfortune, he serenely gave the energies of his mind to the careful survey of the country around.

"During the time that I hunted for them," he writes, "I found the land for a great extent about this river to exceed the soil of Kentucky if possible, and remarkably well watered."

Upon one of the branches of the Scioto River, which stream runs about sixty miles east of the Little Miami, there were some salt springs. Early in June a party of the Indians set out for these "Licks" to make salt. They took

Boone with them. The Indians were quite averse to anything like hard work. Boone not only understood the process of manufacture perfectly, but was always quietly and energetically devoted to whatever he undertook. The Indians, inspired by the double motive of the desire to obtain as much salt as possible, and to hold securely the prisoner, whom they so highly valued, kept him so busy at the kettles as to give him no opportunity to escape.

After an absence of about a fortnight, they returned with a good supply of salt to the Little Miami. Here Boone was quite alarmed to find that during his absence the chiefs had been marshaling a band of four hundred and fifty of their bravest warriors to attack Boonesborough. In that fort were his wife and his children. Its capture would probably insure their slaughter. He was aware that the fort was not sufficiently guarded by its present inmates, and that, unapprehensive of impending danger, they were liable to be taken entirely by surprise. Boone was sufficiently acquainted with the Shawanese dialect to understand every word they said, while he very sagaciously had assumed, from the moment of his captivity, that he was entirely ignorant of their language.

Boone's anxiety was very great. He was compelled to assume a smiling face as he attended their war dances. Apparently unmoved, he listened to the details of their plans for the surprise of the fort. Indeed, to disarm suspicion and to convince them that he had truly become one of their number, he co-operated in giving efficiency to their hostile designs against all he held most dear in the world.

It had now become a matter of infinite moment that he should immediately escape and carry to his friends in the fort the tidings of their peril. But the slightest unwary movement would have led the suspicious Indians so to redouble their vigilance as to render escape utterly impossible. So skilfully did he conceal the emotions which agitated him, and so successfully did he feign entire contentment with his lot, that his captors, all absorbed in the enterprise in which they were engaged, remitted their ordinary vigilance.

On the morning of the sixteenth of June, Boone rose very early to take his usual hunt. With his secreted ammunition, and the amount allowed him by the Indians for the day, he hoped to be able to save himself from starvation, during his flight of five days through the pathless wilderness. There was a distance of one hundred and sixty miles between Old Chilicothe and Boonesborough. The moment his flight should be suspected, four hundred and fifty Indian warriors, breathing vengeance, and in perfect preparation for the pursuit, would be on his track. His capture would almost certainly result in his death by the most cruel tortures; for the infuriated Indians would wreak upon him all their vengeance.

It is however not probable that this silent, pensive man allowed these thoughts seriously to disturb his equanimity. An instinctive trust in God seemed to inspire him. He was forty-three years of age. In the knowledge of wood-craft, and in powers of endurance, no Indian surpassed him. Though he would be pursued by sagacious and veteran warriors and by young Indian braves, a pack of four hundred and fifty savages following with keener scent than that of the bloodhound, one poor victim, yet undismayed, he entered upon the appalling enterprise. The history of the world perhaps presents but few feats so difficult, and yet so successfully performed. And yet the only record which this modest man makes, in his autobiography, of this wonderful adventure is as follows:

> "On the sixteenth, before sunrise, I departed in the most secret manner, and arrived at Boonesborough on the twentieth, after a journey of one hundred and sixty miles, during which I had but one meal."

It was necessary, as soon as Boone got out of sight of the village, to fly with the utmost speed, to put as great a distance as possible between himself and his pursuers, before they should suspect his attempt at escape. He subsequently learned that as soon as the Indians apprehended that he had actually fled, there was the most intense commotion in their camp, and immediately a large number of their fleetest runners and keenest hunters were put upon his trail. He dared not fire a gun. Had he killed any game he could not have ventured to kindle a fire to cook it. He had secretly provided himself with a few cuts of dried venison with which he could appease his hunger as he pressed forward by day and by night, scarcely allowing himself one moment for rest or sleep. His route lay through forests and swamps, and across many streams swollen by recent rains.

At length he reached the Ohio River. Its current was swift and turbid, rolling in a majestic flood half a mile in width, filling the bed of the stream with almost fathomless waters from shore to shore. Experienced as Colonel Boone was in wood-craft, he was not a skilful swimmer. The thought of how he should cross the Ohio had caused him much anxiety. Upon reaching its banks he fortunately—may we not say providentially—found an old canoe which had drifted among the bushes upon the shore. There was a large hole at one end, and it was nearly filled with water. He succeeded in bailing out the water and plugging up the hole, and crossed the river in safety. Then for the first time he so far indulged in a feeling of security as to venture to shoot a turkey, and kindling a fire he feasted abundantly upon the rich repast. It was the only meal in which he indulged during his flight of five days.

On his arrival at Boonesborough, he was welcomed as one risen from the grave. Much to his disappointment he found that his wife with his children, despairing of ever seeing him again, had left the fort and returned to the house of her father, in North Carolina. She supposed that the Indians had killed him. "Oppressed," writes Boone, "with the distresses of the country and bereaved of me, her only happiness, she had undertaken her long and perilous journey through the wilderness." It is gratifying to record that she reached her friends in safety.

Boone found the fort as he had apprehended, in a bad state of defence. His presence, his military skill, and the intelligence he brought, immediately inspired every man to the intensest exertion. The gates were strengthened, new bastions were formed, and provisions were laid in, to stand a siege. Everything was done which could be done to repel an assault from they knew not how many savages, aided by British leaders, for the band from old Chilicothe, was to be joined by warriors from several other tribes. In ten days, Boonesborough was ready for the onset. These arduous labors being completed, Boone heroically resolved to strike consternation into the Indians, by showing them that he was prepared for aggressive as well as defensive warfare, and that they must leave behind them warriors for the protection of their own villages.

Selecting a small party of but nineteen men, about the first of August he emerged from Boonesborough, marched boldly to the Ohio, crossed the river, entered the valley of the Scioto, and was within four miles of an Indian town, Paint Creek, which he intended to destroy, when he chanced to encounter a band of thirty savages painted, thoroughly armed and on the war path, to join the band advancing from Old Chilicothe. The Indians were attacked with such vehemence by Boone, that they fled in consternation, leaving behind them three horses and all their baggage. The savages also lost one killed and two wounded, while they inflicted no loss whatever upon the white men.

Boone sent forward some swift runners as spies, and they speedily returned with the report that the Indians in a panic had entirely abandoned Paint Creek. Aware that the warriors would rush to join the four hundred and fifty from Old Chilicothe, and that they might cut off his retreat, or reach Boonesborough before his return, he immediately commenced a rapid movement back to the fort. Every man would be needed there for an obstinate defence. This foray had extended one hundred and fifty miles from the fort. It greatly alarmed the Indians. It emboldened the hearts of the garrison, and gave them intelligence of the approach of their foes. After an absence of but seven days, Boone with his heroic little band quite triumphantly re-entered the fort.

The approach of the foe is described in the following terms by Boone:

> "On the eighth of August, the Indian army arrived, being four hundred and forty-four in number, commanded by Captain Duquesne, eleven other Frenchmen and some of their own chiefs, and marched up in view of our fort, with British and French colors flying. And having sent a summons to me in His Britannic Majesty's name to surrender the fort, I requested two days' consideration which was granted. It was now a critical period with us. We were a small number in the garrison; a powerful army before our walls, whose appearance proclaimed inevitable death; fearfully painted and marking their footsteps with desolation.

Death was preferable to captivity; and if taken by storm, we must inevitably be devoted to destruction.

"In this situation we concluded to maintain our garrison if possible. We immediately proceeded to collect what we could of our horses and other cattle, and bring them through the posterns into the fort; and in the evening of the ninth, I returned the answer 'that we were determined to defend our fort while a man was living.'

"'Now,' said I to their commander who stood attentively hearing my sentiments, 'we laugh at your formidable preparations, but thank you for giving us notice, and time for our defence. Your efforts will not prevail, for our gates shall forever deny you admittance.'

"Whether this answer affected their courage or not, I cannot tell, but contrary to our expectations, they formed a scheme to deceive us, declaring it was their orders from Governor Hamilton to take us captives, and not to destroy us; but if nine of us would come out and treat with them, they would immediately withdraw their forces from our walls, and return home peaceably. This sounded grateful in our ears, and we agreed to the proposal."

Chapter 9

VICTORIES AND DEFEATS

There were but fifty men in the garrison at Boonesborough. They were assailed by a body of more than ten to one of the bravest Indian warriors, under the command of an officer in the British army. The boldest in the fort felt that their situation was almost desperate. The ferocity of the Indian, and the intelligence of the white man, were combined against them. They knew that the British commander, however humane he might be, would have no power, should the fort be taken by storm, to save them from death by the most horrible tortures.

General Duquesne was acting under instructions from Governor Hamilton, the British officer in supreme command at Detroit. Boone knew that the Governor felt very kindly towards him. When he had been carried to that place a captive, the Governor had made very earnest endeavors to obtain his liberation. Influenced by these considerations, he consented to hold the conference.

But, better acquainted with the Indian character than perhaps Duquesne could have been, he selected nine of the most athletic and strong of the garrison, and appointed the place of meeting in front of the fort, at a distance of only one hundred and twenty feet from the walls. The riflemen of the garrison were placed in a position to cover the spot with their guns, so that in case of treachery the Indians would meet with instant punishment, and the retreat of the party from the fort would probably be secured. The language of Boone is:

> "We held a treaty within sixty yards of the garrison on purpose to divert them from a breach of honor, as we could not avoid suspicion of the savages."

The terms proposed by General Duquesne were extremely liberal. And while they might satisfy the British party, whose object in the war was simply to conquer the colonists and bring them back to loyalty, they could by no means have satisfied the Indians, who desired not merely to drive the white men back from their hunting grounds, but to plunder them of their possessions and to gratify their savage natures by hearing the shrieks of their victims at the stake and by carrying home the trophies of numerous scalps.

Boone and his men, buried in the depths of the wilderness, had probably taken little interest in the controversy which was just then rising between the colonies and the mother country. They had regarded the King of England as their lawful sovereign, and their minds had never been agitated by the question of revolution or of independence. When, therefore, General Duquesne proposed that they should take the oath of allegiance to the King of Great Britain, and that then they should be permitted to return unmolested to their homes and their friends beyond the mountains, taking all their possessions with them, Colonel Boone and his associates were very ready to accept such terms. It justly appeared to them in their isolated condition, five hundred miles away from the Atlantic coast, that this was vastly preferable to remaining in the wilderness assailed by thousands of Indians guided by English energy and abundantly provided with all the munitions of war from British arsenals.

But Boone knew very well that the Indians would never willingly assent to this treaty. Still he and his fellow commissioners signed it while very curious to learn how it would be regarded by their savage foes. The commissioners on both sides had appeared at the appointed place of conference, as is usual on such occasions, entirely unarmed. There were, however, a large number of Indians lingering around and drawing nearer as the conference proceeded. After the treaty was signed, the old Indian chief Blackfish, Boone's adopted father, and who, exasperated by the escape of his ungrateful son, had been watching him with a very unamiable expression of countenance, arose and made a formal speech in the most approved style of Indian eloquence. He commented upon the bravery of the two armies, and of the desirableness that there should be entire friendship between them, and closed by saying that it was a custom with them on all such important occasions to ratify the treaty by two Indians shaking hands with each white man.

This shallow pretense, scarcely up to the sagacity of children, by which Blackfish hoped that two savages grappling each one of the commissioners would easily be able to make prisoners of them, and then by threats of torture compel the surrender of the fort, did not in the slightest degree deceive Colonel Boone. He was well aware of his own strength and of that of the men who accompanied him. He also knew that his riflemen occupied concealed positions, from which, with unerring aim, they could instantly punish the savages for any act of treachery. He therefore consented to the arrangement. The grasp was given. Instantly a terrible scene of confusion ensued.

The burly savages tried to drag off their victims. The surrounding Indians rushed in to their aid, and a deadly fire was opened upon them from the fort, which was energetically responded to by all the armed savages from behind stumps and trees. One of the fiercest of battles had instantly blazed forth. Still these stalwart pioneers were not taken by surprise. Aided by the bullets of the fort, they shook off their assailants, and all succeeded in escaping within the heavy gates, which were immediately closed behind them. One only of their number, Boone's brother, was wounded. This escape seems almost miraculous. But the majority of the Indians in intelligence were mere children: sometimes very cunning, but often with the grossest stupidity mingled with their strategy.

Duquesne and Blackfish, the associated leaders, now commenced the siege of the fort with all their energies. Dividing their forces into two parties, they kept up an incessant fire upon the garrison for nine days and nine nights. It was one of the most heroic of those bloody struggles between civilization and barbarism, which have rendered the plains of Kentucky memorable.

The savages were very careful not to expose themselves to the rifles of the besieged. They were stationed behind rocks, and trees, and stumps, so that it was seldom that the garrison could catch even a glimpse of the foes who were assailing them. It was necessary for those within the fort to be sparing of their ammunition. They seldom fired unless they could take deliberate aim, and then the bullet was almost always sure to reach its mark. Colonel Boone, in describing this attempt of the Indians to capture the commissioners by stratagem, and of the storm of war which followed, writes:

> "They immediately grappled us, but, although surrounded by hundreds of savages, we extricated ourselves from them and escaped all safe into the garrison except one, who was wounded through a heavy fire from their army. They immediately attacked us on every side, and a constant heavy fire ensued between us, day and night, for the space of nine days. In this time the enemy began to undermine our fort, which was situated about sixty yards from the Kentucky River. They began at the water mark and proceeded in the bank some distance, which we understood by their making the water muddy with the clay. We immediately proceeded to disappoint their design by cutting a trench across their subterranean passage. The enemy discovering our counter mine by the clay we threw out of the fort, desisted from that stratagem. Experience now fully convincing them that neither their power nor their policy could effect their purpose, on the twentieth of August they raised the siege and departed.
>
> "During this siege, which threatened death in every form, we had two men killed and four wounded, besides a number of cattle. We killed of the enemy thirty-seven and wounded a great number. After they were gone we picked up one hundred and twenty-five pounds weight of bullets, besides what stuck in the logs of our fort, which certainly is a great proof of their industry."

It is said that during this siege, one of the negroes, probably a slave, deserted from the fort with one of their best rifles, and joined the Indians. Concealing himself in a tree, where unseen he could take deliberate aim, he became one of the most successful of the assailants. But the eagle eye of Boone detected him, and though, as was afterwards ascertained by actual measurement, the tree was five hundred and twenty-five feet distant from the fort, Boone took deliberate aim, fired, and the man was seen to drop heavily from his covert to the ground. The bullet from Boone's rifle had pierced his brain.

At one time the Indians had succeeded in setting fire to the fort, by throwing flaming combustibles upon it, attached to their arrows. One of the young men extinguished the flames, exposing himself to the concentrated and deadly fire of the assailants in doing so. Though the bullets fell like hailstones around him, the brave fellow escaped unscathed.

This repulse quite disheartened the Indians. Henceforth they regarded Boonesborough as a Gibraltar; impregnable to any force which they could bring against it. They never assailed it again. Though Boonesborough is now but a small village in Kentucky, it has a history which will render it forever memorable in the annals of heroism.

It will be remembered that Boone's family, supposing him to have perished by the hands of the Indians, had returned to the home of Mrs. Boone's father in North Carolina. Colonel Boone, anxious to rejoin his wife and children, and feeling that Boonesborough was safe from any immediate attack by the Indians, soon after the dispersion of the savages entered again upon the long journey through the wilderness, to find his friends east of the mountains. In the autumn of 1778, Colonel Boone again found himself, after all his wonderful adventures, in a peaceful home on the banks of the Yadkin.

The settlements in Kentucky continued rapidly to increase. The savages had apparently relinquished all hope of holding exclusive possession of the country. Though there were occasional acts of violence and cruelty, there was quite a truce in the Indian warfare. But the white settlers, and those who wished to emigrate, were greatly embarrassed by conflicting land claims. Many of the pioneers found their titles pronounced to be of no validity. Others who wished to emigrate, experienced great difficulty in obtaining secure possession of their lands. The reputation of Kentucky as in all respects one of the most desirable of earthly regions for comfortable homes, added to the desire of many families to escape from the horrors of revolutionary war, which was sweeping the sea-board, led to a constant tide of emigration beyond the mountains.

Under these circumstances the Government of Virginia established a court, consisting of four prominent citizens, to go from place to place, examine such titles as should be presented to them, and to confirm those which were good. This commission commenced its duties at St. Asaph. All the old terms of settlement proposed by Henderson and the Transylvania Company were abrogated. Thus Colonel Boone had no title to a single acre of land in Kentucky. A new law however was enacted as follows:

> "Any person may acquire title to so much unappropriated land, as he or she may desire to purchase, on paying the consideration of forty pounds for every one hundred acres, and so in proportion."

This money was to be paid to the State Treasurer, who would give for it a receipt. This receipt was to be deposited with the State Auditor, who would in exchange for it give a certificate. This certificate was to be lodged at the Land Office. There it was to be registered, and a warrant was to be given, authorizing the survey of the land selected. Surveyors who had passed the ordeal of William and Mary College, having defined the boundaries of the land, were to make a return to the Land Office. A due record was there to be made of the survey, a deed was to be given in the name of the State, which deed was to be signed by the Governor, with the seal of the Commonwealth attached.

This was a perplexing labyrinth for the pioneer to pass through, before he could get a title to his land. Not only Colonel Boone, but it seems that his family were anxious to return to the beautiful fields of Kentucky. During the few months he remained on the Yadkin, he was busy in converting every particle of property he possessed into money, and in raising every dollar he could for the purchase of lands he so greatly desired. The sum he obtained amounted to about twenty thousand dollars, in the depreciated paper currency of that day. To Daniel Boone this was a large sum. With this the simple-hearted man started for Richmond to pay it to the State Treasurer, and to obtain for it the promised certificate. He was also entrusted with quite large sums of money from his neighbors, for a similar purpose.

On his way he was robbed of every dollar. It was a terrible blow to him, for it not only left him penniless, but exposed him to the insinuation of having feigned the robbery, that he might retain the money entrusted to him by his friends. Those who knew Daniel Boone well would have no more suspected him of fraud than an angel of light. With others however, his character suffered. Rumor was busy in denouncing him.

Colonel Nathaniel Hart had entrusted Boone with two thousand nine hundred pounds. This of course was all gone. A letter, however, is preserved from Colonel Hart, which bears noble testimony to the character of the man from whom he had suffered:

> "I observe what you say respecting our losses by Daniel Boone. I had heard of the misfortune soon after it happened, but not of my being a partaker before now. I feel for the poor people who perhaps are to lose their pre-emptions. But I must say I feel more for Boone, whose character I am told suffers by it. Much degenerated must the people of this age be, when amongst them are to be found men to censure and blast the reputation of a person so just and upright, and in whose breast is a seat of virtue too pure to admit of a thought so base and dishonorable. I have known Boone in times of old, when poverty and distress had him fast by the hand, and in these wretched circumstances, I have ever found him of a noble and generous soul, despising everything mean, and therefore I will freely grant him a discharge for whatever sums of mine he might have been possessed at the time."

Boone was now forty-five years of age, but the hardships to which he had been exposed had borne heavily upon him, and he appeared ten years older. Though he bore without a murmur the loss of his earthly all, and the imputations which were cast upon his character, he was more anxious than ever to find refuge from the embarrassments which oppressed him in the solitudes of his beautiful Kentucky. Notwithstanding his comparative poverty, his family on the banks of the Yadkin need not experience any want. Land was fertile, abundant and cheap. He and his boys in a few days, with their axes, could erect as good a house as they desired to occupy. The cultivation of a few acres of the soil, and the results of the chase, would provide them an ample support. Here also they could retire to rest at night, with unbolted door and with no fear that their slumbers would be disturbed by the yell of the blood-thirsty savage.

The wife and mother must doubtless have wished to remain in her pleasant home, but cheerfully and nobly she acceded to his wishes, and was ready to accompany him to all the abounding perils of the distant West. Again the family set out on its journey across the mountains. Of the incidents which they encountered, we are not informed. The narrative we have from Boone is simply as follows: our readers will excuse the slight repetition it involves:

> "About this time I returned to Kentucky with my family. And here, to avoid an enquiry into my conduct, the reader being before informed of my bringing my family to Kentucky, I am under the necessity of informing him that during my captivity with the Indians, my wife, who despaired of ever seeing me again, had transported my family and goods back through the wilderness, amid a multitude of dangers, to her father's house in North Carolina. Shortly after the troubles at Boonesborough, I went to them and lived peaceably there until this time. The history of my going home and returning with my family forms a series of difficulties, an account of which would swell a volume. And being foreign to my purpose I shall omit them."

During Boone's absence from Kentucky, one of the most bloody battles was fought, which ever occurred between the whites and the Indians. Colonel Rogers, returning with supplies (by boat) from New Orleans to the Upper Ohio, when he arrived at the mouth of the Little Miami, detected the Indians in large numbers, painted, armed, and evidently on the war path, emerging from the mouth of the river in their canoes, and crossing the

Ohio to the Kentucky shore. He cautiously landed his men, intending to attack the Indians by surprise. Instead of this, they turned upon him with overwhelming numbers, and assailed him with the greatest fury. Colonel Rogers and sixty of his men were almost instantly killed. This constituted nearly the whole of his party. Two or three effected their escape, and conveyed the sad tidings of the massacre to the settlements.

The Kentuckians were exceedingly exasperated, and resolved that the Indians should feel the weight of their vengeance. Colonel Bowman, in accordance with a custom of the times, issued a call, inviting all the Kentuckians who were willing to volunteer under his leadership for the chastisement of the Indians, to rendezvous at Harrodsburg. Three hundred determined men soon assembled. The expedition moved in the month of July, and commenced the ascent of the Little Miami undiscovered. They arrived in the vicinity of Old Chilicothe just before nightfall. Here it was determined so to arrange their forces in the darkness, as to attack the place just before the dawn of the ensuing day. One half of the army, under the command of Colonel Logan, were to grope their way through the woods, and march around the town so as to attack it in the rear, at a given signal from Colonel Bowman, who was to place his men in position for efficient cooperation. Logan accomplished his movement, and concealing his men behind stumps, trees, and rocks, anxiously awaited the signal for attack.

But the sharp ear of a watch-dog detected some unusual movement, and commenced barking furiously. An Indian warrior came from his cabin, and cautiously advanced the way the dog seemed to designate. As the Indian drew near, one of the party, by accident or great imprudence, discharged his gun. The Indian gave a war-whoop, which immediately startled all the inmates of the cabins to their feet. Logan and his party were sufficiently near to see the women and the children in a continuous line rushing over the ridge, to the protection of the forest.

The Indian warriors, with a military discipline hardly to be expected of them, instantly collected in several strong cabins, which were their citadels, and from whose loop-holes, unexposed, they could open a deadly fire upon their assailants, In an instant, the whole aspect of affairs was changed. The assailants advancing through the clearing, must expose their unprotected breasts to the bullets of an unseen foe. After a brief conflict, Colonel Logan, to his bitter disappointment and that of his men, felt constrained to order a retreat.

The two parties were soon reunited, having lost several valuable lives, and depressed by the conviction that the enterprise had proved an utter failure. The savages pursued, keeping up a harassing fire upon the rear of the fugitives. Fortunately for the white men, the renowned Indian chieftain Blackfish, struck by a bullet, was instantly killed. This so disheartened his followers, that they abandoned the pursuit. The fugitives continued their flight all the night, and then at their leisure returned to their homes much dejected. In this disastrous expedition, nine men were killed and one was severely wounded.

The Indians, aided by their English allies, resolved by the invasion of Kentucky to retaliate for the invasion of the Little Miami. Governor Hamilton raised a very formidable army, and supplied them with two pieces of artillery. By such weapons the strongest log fort could speedily be demolished; while the artillerists would be entirely beyond the reach of the guns of the garrison. A British officer, Colonel Boyd, commanded the combined force. The valley of the Licking River, along whose banks many thriving settlements had commenced, was their point of destination.

A twelve days' march from the Ohio brought this army, which was considered a large one in those times, to a post called Kuddle's Station. The garrison was immediately summoned to surrender, with the promise of protection for their lives only. Resistance against artillery was hopeless. The place was surrendered. Indians and white men rushed in, alike eager for plunder. The Indians, breaking loose from all restraint, caught men, women and children, and claimed them as their prisoners. Three persons who made some slight resistance were immediately tomahawked.

The British commander endeavored to exonerate himself from these atrocities by saying that it was utterly beyond his power to control the savages. These wolfish allies, elated by their conquest, their plunder and their captives, now demanded to be led along the valley five miles to the next station, called Martin's Fort. It is said that Colonel Byrd was so affected by the uncontrollable atrocities he had witnessed, that he refused to continue the expedition, unless the Indians would consent, that while they should receive all the plunder, he should have all the prisoners. It is also said that notwithstanding this agreement, the same scenes were enacted at Martin's Fort which had been witnessed at Ruddle's Station. In confirmation of this statement, it is certain that Colonel Byrd refused to go any farther. All the stations on the river were apparently at his disposal, and it speaks well for his humanity that he refused to lead any farther savages armed with the tomahawk and the scalping knife, against his white brethren. He could order a retreat, as he did, but he could not rescue the captives from those who had seized them. The Indians loaded down their victims with the plunder of their own dwellings, and as they fell by the way, sinking beneath their burdens, they buried the tomahawk in their brains.

The exasperation on both sides was very great, and General Clark, who was stationed at Fort Jefferson with a thousand picked men, entered the Indian territory, burned the villages, destroyed the crops, and utterly devastated the country. In reference to this expedition, Mr. Cecil B. Hartley writes:

> "Some persons who have not the slightest objection to war, very gravely express doubts as to whether the expedient of destroying the crops of the Indians was justifiable. It is generally treated by these men as if it were a wanton display of a vindictive spirit, where in reality it was dictated by the soundest policy; for when the Indians' harvests were destroyed, they were compelled to subsist their families altogether by hunting, and had no leisure for their murderous inroads into the settlements. This result was plainly seen on this occasion, for it does not appear that the Indians attacked any of the settlements during the remainder of this year."

The following incident, well authenticated, which occurred early in the spring of 1780, gives one a vivid idea of the nature of this warfare:

> "Mr. Alexander McConnel of Lexington, while out hunting, killed a large buck. He went home for his horse to bring it in. While he was

absent, five Indians accidentally discovered the body of the deer. Supposing the hunter would return, three of them hid themselves within rifle shot of the carcass while two followed his trail. McConnel, anticipating no danger, was riding slowly along the path, when he was fired upon from ambush, his horse shot beneath him, and he seized as a prisoner. His captors were in high glee, and treated him with unusual kindness. His skill with the rifle excited their admiration, and as he provided them with abundance of game, they soon became quite fond of him. Day after day the savages continued their tramp to the Ohio River, to cross over to their own country. Every night they bound him very strongly. As they became better acquainted, and advanced farther from the settlements of the pioneers, they in some degree remitted their vigilance. One evening when they had arrived near the Ohio, McConnel complained so earnestly of the pain which the tightly bound cords gave him, that they more loosely fastened the cord of buffalo hide around his wrists. Still they tied it, as they supposed securely, and attached the end of the cord to the body of one of the Indians.

"At midnight, McConnel discovered a sharp knife lying near him, which had accidentally fallen from its sheath. He drew it to him with his feet, and succeeded noiselessly in cutting the cords. Still he hardly dared to stir, for there was danger that the slightest movement might rouse his vigilant foes. The savages had stacked their five guns near the fire. Cautiously he crept towards them, and secreted three at but a short distance where they would not easily find them. He then crept noiselessly back, took a rifle in each hand, rested the muzzles upon a log, and aiming one at the heart, and one at the head of two Indians at the distance of a few feet, discharged both guns simultaneously.

"Both shots were fatal. The three remaining savages in bewilderment sprang to their feet. McConnel instantly seizing the two other guns, shot one through the heart, and inflicted a terrible wound upon the other. He fell to the ground bellowing loudly. Soon however he regained his feet and hobbled off into the woods as fast as possible. The only remaining one of the party who was unhurt uttered a loud yell of terror and dismay, and bounded like a deer into the forest. McConnel was not disposed to remain even for one moment to contemplate the result of his achievement. He selected his own trusty rifle, plunged into the forest, and with the unerring instinct of the veteran hunter, in two days reached the garrison at Lexington to relate to them his wonderful escape."

Chapter 10

BRITISH ALLIES

It was in the autumn of the year 1780 that Daniel Boone, with his family, returned to Boonesborough. A year before, the Legislature of Virginia had recognized essentially what is now Kentucky as one of the counties of Virginia, and had established the town of Boonesborough as its capital. By this act Daniel Boone was named one of the trustees or selectmen. Town lots were ordered to be surveyed, and a very liberal grant of land was conferred upon everyone who would erect a house at least sixteen feet square, with either brick, stone, or dirt chimney. For some reason Colonel Boone declined this office. It is probable that he was disgusted by his own experience in the civil courts.

There was little danger now of an attack upon Boonesborough by the Indians. There were so many settlements around it that no foe could approach without due warning and without encountering serious opposition. On the sixth of October Daniel Boone, with his brother Squire, left the fort alone for what would seem to be an exceedingly imprudent excursion, so defenceless, to the Blue Licks. They reached the Licks in safety. While there they were discovered by a party of Indians, and were fired upon from ambush. Squire Boone was instantly killed and scalped. Daniel, heart-stricken by the loss of his beloved brother, fled like a deer, pursued by the whole band, filling the forest with their yells like a pack of hounds. The Indians had a very powerful dog with them, who, with unerring scent, followed closely in the trail of the fugitive. For three miles this unequal chase continued. The dog, occasionally embarrassed in his pursuit, would be delayed for a time in regaining the trail. The speed of Boone was such that the foremost of the savages was left far behind. He then, as the dog came bounding on, stopped, took deliberate aim, and shot the brute.

Boone was still far from the fort, but he reached it in safety, leaving upon the Indians the impression that he bore a charmed life. He was very deeply afflicted by the death of his brother. Squire was the youngest of the sons, and the tie which bound the brothers together was unusually tender and confidential. They had shared in many perilous adventures, and for months had dwelt entirely alone in the wilderness, far away from any other society.

The winter of 1780 was one of the saddest in the annals of our country. The colonial army, everywhere defeated, was in the most deplorable state of destitution and suffering. Our frontiers were most cruelly ravaged by a barbarian foe. To add to all this, the winter was severely cold, beyond any precedent. The crops had been so destroyed by the enemy that many of the pioneers were compelled to live almost entirely upon the flesh of the buffalo.

Virginia, in extending her jurisdiction over her western lands of Kentucky, now, for the sake of a more perfect military organization, divided the extensive region into three counties—Fayette, Lincoln, and Jefferson. General Clarke was made commander-in-chief of the Kentucky militia. Daniel Boone was commissioned as Lieutenant-Colonel of Lincoln County. The emigration into the State at this time may be inferred from the fact that the Court of Commissioners to examine land titles, at the close of its session of seven months had granted three thousand claims. Its meetings had been held mainly at Boonesborough, and its labors terminated in April, 1780. During the spring three hundred barges, loaded with emigrants, were floated down the Ohio to the Falls, at what is now Louisville.

As we have stated, the winter had been one of the most remarkable on record. From the middle of November to the middle of February, the ground was covered with snow and ice, without a thaw. The severity of the cold was terrible. Nearly all unprotected animals perished. Even bears, buffalo, wolves, and wild turkeys were found frozen in the woods. The starving wild animals often came near the settlement for food. For seventy-five years the winter of 1780 was an era to which the old men referred.

Though the Indians organized no formidable raids, they were very annoying. No one could safely wander any distance from the forts. In March, 1781, several bands entered Jefferson County, and by lying in ambush killed four of the settlers. Captain Whittaker, with fifteen men, went in pursuit of them. He followed their trail to the banks of the Ohio. Supposing they had crossed, he and his party embarked in canoes, boldly to continue the pursuit into the Indian country. They had scarcely pushed a rod from the shore when hideous yells rose from the Indians in ambush, and a deadly fire was opened upon the canoes. Nine of the pioneers were instantly killed or wounded. The savages, having accomplished this feat, fled into the wilderness, where the party, thus weakened in numbers, could not pursue them.

A small party of settlers had reared their log-huts near the present site of Shelbyville. Squire Boone had been one of the prominent actors in the establishment of this little colony. Alarmed by the menaces of the savages, these few settlers decided to remove to a more secure station on Bear's Creek. On their way they were startled by the war-whoop of they knew not how many Indians concealed in ambush, and a storm of bullets fell upon them, killing and wounding many of their number. The miscreants, scarcely waiting for the return fire, fled with yells which resounded through the forest, leaving their victims to the sad task of burying the dead and nursing the wounded. Colonel Floyd collected twenty-five men to pursue them. The wary Indians, nearly two hundred in number, drew them into an ambush and opened upon the party a deadly fire which almost instantly killed half their number. The remainder with great difficulty escaped, leaving their dead to be mutilated by the scalping knife of the savage.

Almost every day brought tidings of similar disasters. The Indians, emboldened by these successes, seemed to rouse themselves to a new determination to exterminate the whites. The conduct of the British Government, in calling such wretches to their alliance in their war with the colonies, created the greatest exasperation. Thomas Jefferson gave expression to the public sentiment in the Declaration of Independence, in which he says, in arraignment of King George the Third:

> "He has endeavored to bring on the inhabitants of our frontiers the merciless Indian savages, whose known rule of warfare is an undistinguished destruction of all ages, sexes, and conditions."

There were two wretched men, official agents of the British Government, who were more savage than the savages themselves. One of them, a vagabond named Simon Gerty, had joined the Indians by adoption. He had not only acquired their habits, but had become their leader in the most awful scenes of ferocity. He was a tory, and as such was the bitterest foe of the colonists, who were struggling for independence. The other, Colonel McGee, with a little more respectability of character, was equally fiendlike in exciting the Indians to the most revolting barbarities. Thus incited and sustained by British authority, the Indians kept all the settlers in Kentucky in constant alarm.

Instigated by the authorities at Detroit, the warriors of five tribes assembled at Old Chilicothe to organize the most formidable expedition which had as yet invaded Kentucky. These tribes were the Shawanese on the Little Miami, the Cherokees on the Tennessee, the Wyandotts on the Sandusky, the Tawas on the Maumee, and the Delawares on the Muskingum.

Their choicest warriors, five hundred in number, rendezvoused at Old Chilicothe. This Indian village was built in the form of a square enclosing a large area. Some of their houses were of logs, some of bark, some of reeds filled in with clay. Boone says that the Indians concentrated their utmost force and vengeance upon this expedition, hoping to destroy the settlements and to depopulate the country at a single blow.

Not far from Boonesborough, in the same valley of the Kentucky, there was a small settlement called Bryant's Station. William Bryant, the founder, had married a sister of Colonel Boone. On the fifteenth of August, a war party of five hundred Indians and Canadians, under the leadership of Simon Gerty, appeared before this little cluster of log-huts, each of which was of course bullet-proof. The settlers fought heroically. Gerty was wounded, and thirty of his band were killed, while the garrison lost but four. The assailing party, thus disappointed in their expectation of carrying the place by storm, and fearing the arrival of reinforcements from other settlements, hastily retired. Colonel Boone, hearing of the attack, hastened to the rescue, joining troops from several of the adjacent forts. The party consisted of one hundred and eighty men, under the leadership of Colonel Todd, one of "nature's noblemen." Colonel Boone seems to have been second in command. Two of his sons, Israel and Samuel, accompanied their father upon this expedition.

The Indians, led by British officers, were far more to be dreaded than when left to their own cunning, which was often childish. As the little band of pioneers, rushing to the rescue, approached Bryant's Station and were informed of the retreat of the invaders, a council of war was held, to decide whether it were best for a hundred and eighty men to pursue five hundred Indians and Canadians, through a region where every mile presented the most favorable opportunities for concealment in ambush. Gerty was a desperado who was to be feared as well as hated. Contrary to the judgment of both Colonels Todd and Boone, it was decided to pursue the Indians. There was no difficulty in following the trail of so large a band, many of whom were mounted. Their path led almost directly north, to the Licking River, and then followed down its banks towards the Ohio.

As the pursuers were cautiously advancing, they came to a remarkable bend in the stream, where there was a large and open space, with prairie grass very high. A well trampled buffalo track led through this grass, which was almost like a forest of reeds. Along this "street" the Indians had retreated. The scouts who had been sent forward to explore, returned with the report that there were no signs of Indians. And yet, four hundred savages had so adroitly concealed themselves, that their line really extended from bank to bank of the river, where it bent like a horseshoe before them. The combined cunning of the Indian, and the intelligence of their white leaders, was now fatally enlisted for the destruction of the settlers. A hundred and eighty men were to be caught in a trap, with five hundred demons prepared to shoot them down.

As soon as Colonel Todd's party passed the neck of this bend, the Indians closed in behind them, rose from their concealment, and with terrific yells opened upon them a still more terrific fire. The pioneers fought with the courage of desperation. At the first discharge, nearly one third of Colonel Todd's little party fell dead or wounded. Struck fatally by several bullets, Colonel Todd himself fell from his horse drenched with blood. While a portion of the Indians kept up the fire, others, with hideous yells sprang forward with tomahawk and scalping knife, completing their fiendlike work. It was a scene of awful confusion and dismay. The survivors fighting every step of the way, retreated towards the river, for there was no escape back through their thronging foes. Colonel Boone's two sons fought by the side of their father. Samuel, the younger, struck by a bullet, was severely but not mortally wounded. Israel, his second son, fell dead. The unhappy father, took his dead boy upon his shoulders to save him from the scalping knife. As he tottered beneath the bleeding body, an Indian of herculean stature with uplifted tomahawk rushed upon him. Colonel Boone dropped the body of his son, shot the Indian through the heart, and seeing the savages rushing upon him from all directions, fled, leaving the corpse of his boy to its fate.

Being intimately acquainted with the ground, he plunged into a ravine, baffling several parties who pursued him, swam across the river, and entering the forest succeeded in escaping from his foes, and at length safely by a circuitous route returned to Bryant's Station. In the meantime the scene of tumult and slaughter was awful beyond all description. Victors and vanquished were blended together upon the banks of the stream. In this dreadful conflict there were four Indians to each white man. There was a narrow ford at the spot, but the whole stream seemed clogged, some swimming and some trying to wade, while the exultant Indians shot and tomahawked without mercy. Those who succeeded in crossing the river, leaving the great buffalo track which they had been following, plunged into the thickets, and though vigorously pursued by the Indians, most of them eventually reached the settlements.

In this dreadful disaster, the colonists lost sixty men in killed and seven were taken prisoners. The Indians in counting up their loss, found that sixty-four were missing. In accordance with their barbaric custom, they selected in vengeance four of the prisoners and put them to death by the most terrible tortures which savage ingenuity could devise. Had Colonel Boone's advice been followed, this calamity might have been avoided. Still characteristically, he uttered not a word of complaint. In his comments upon the event he says:

> "I cannot reflect upon this dreadful scene but sorrow fills my heart. A zeal for the defence of their country led these heroes to the scene of action, though with a few men to attack a powerful army of experienced warriors. When we gave way, they pursued us with the utmost eagerness, and in every quarter spread destruction. The river was difficult to cross, and many were killed in the flight; some just entering the river, some in the water, others after crossing, in ascending the cliffs. Some escaped on horseback, a few on foot; and being dispersed everywhere in a few hours, brought the melancholy news of this unfortunate conflict to Lexington. The reader may guess what sorrow filled the hearts of the inhabitants; exceeding anything I am able to describe. Being reinforced we returned to bury the dead, and found their bodies strewed everywhere, cut and mangled in a dreadful manner. This mournful scene exhibited a horror almost unparalleled; some torn and eaten by wild beasts; those in the river eaten by fishes; all in such a putrified condition that no one could be distinguished from another."

This battle of the Blue Licks, as it is called, occupies one of the most mournful pages in the history of Kentucky. The escape of Boone adds another to the extraordinary adventures of this chivalric and now sorrow-stricken man. Colonel Boone communicated an official report to the Governor of Virginia, Benjamin Harrison, father of William Henry Harrison, subsequently President of the United States. In this report, it is noticeable that Boone makes no allusion whatever to his own services.

This modest document throws such light upon the character of this remarkable man, and upon the peril of the times, that it merits full insertion here. It is as follows:

"Boone's Station, Fayette Co., Aug. 30, 1782.

"Sir,—Present circumstances of affairs cause me to write to Your Excellency, as follows: On the sixteenth instant, a large body of Indians, with some white men, attacked one of our frontier stations, known as Bryant's Station. The siege continued from about sunrise until two o'clock of the next day, when they marched off. Notice being given to the neighboring stations, we immediately raised one hundred and eighty-one horsemen, commanded by Col. John Todd, including some of the Lincoln County militia, and pursued about forty miles."

After a brief account of the battle which we have already given, he continues:

"Afterwards we were reinforced by Colonel Logan, which made our force four hundred and sixty men. We marched again to the battle ground, but finding the enemy had gone, we proceeded to bury the dead. We found forty-three on the ground, and many lay about which we could not stay to find, hungry and weary as we were, and dubious that the enemy might not have gone off quite. By the sign, we thought that the Indians exceeded four hundred, while the whole of the militia of the county does not amount to more than one hundred and thirty.

"From these facts, Your Excellency may form an idea of our situation. I know that your own circumstances are critical; but are we to be wholly forgotten? I hope not. I trust that about five hundred men may be sent to our assistance immediately. If these shall be stationed as our county lieutenant shall deem necessary, it may be the means of saving our part of the country. But if they are placed under the direction of General Clarke, they will be of little or no service to our settlement. The Falls lie one hundred miles west of us, and the Indians north-east; while our men are frequently called to protect them.

"I have encouraged the people in this county all that I could; but I can no longer justify them or myself to risk our lives here, under such extraordinary hazards. The inhabitants of this county are very much alarmed at the thoughts of the Indians bringing another campaign into our country this fall. If this should be the case, it will break up these settlements. I hope therefore that Your Excellency will take the matter into your consideration, and send us some relief as quick as possible. These are my sentiments without consulting any person. Colonel Logan will I expect immediately send you an express, by whom I humbly request Your Excellency's answer. In the meantime, I remain yours, etc., Daniel Boone."

General Clarke, who was the military leader of Kentucky under the Colonial government, was established at *the Falls*. The British authorities held their head-quarters at Detroit, from which post they were sending out their Indian allies in all directions to ravage the frontiers. General Clarke was a man of great energy of character, and he was anxious to organise an expedition against Detroit. With this object in view, he had by immense exertions assembled a force of nearly two thousand men. Much to his chagrin, he received orders to remain at the Falls for the present, to protect the frontiers then so severely menaced. But when the tidings reached him of the terrible disaster at the Blue Lick, he resolved to pursue the Indians and punish them with the greatest severity.

The exultant savages had returned to Old Chilicothe, and had divided their spoil and their captives. Colonel Boone was immediately sent for to take part in this expedition. Clarke's army crossed the Ohio, and marching very rapidly up the banks of the Little Miami, arrived within two miles of Chilicothe before they were discovered. On perceiving the enemy the Indians scattered in all directions. Men, women and children fled into the remote forest, abandoning their homes and leaving everything behind them. The avenging army swept the valley with fire and ruin. Their corn just ripening, and upon which they mainly relied for their winter supply of food, was utterly destroyed. Every tree which bore any fruit was felled, and five of their towns were laid in ashes. The trail of the army presented a scene of utter desolation.

The savages were alike astonished and dismayed. They had supposed that the white men, disheartened by their dreadful defeat at the Blue Lick, would abandon the country. Instead of that, with amazing recuperative power, they had scarcely reached their homes where another army, utterly resistless in numbers, is burning their towns and destroying their whole country.

This avenging campaign so depressed the Indians that they made no farther attempt for the organised invasion of Kentucky. The termination of the war with England also deprived them of their military resources, and left them to their own unaided and unintelligent efforts. Still miserable bands continued prowling around, waylaying and murdering the lonely traveler, setting fire to the solitary hut and inflicting such other outrages as were congenial with their cruel natures. It thus became necessary for the pioneers always to live with the rifle in hand.

Colonel Boone had become especially obnoxious to the Indians. Twice he had escaped from them, under circumstances which greatly mortified their vanity. They recognised the potency of his rifle in the slaughter of their own warriors at the Blue Lick; and they were well aware that it was his sagacity which led the army of General Clarke in its avenging march through their country. It thus became with them an object of intense desire to take him prisoner, and had he been taken, he would doubtless have been doomed to the severest torture they could inflict.

Mr. Peck, in his interesting life of Boone, gives the following account of one of the extraordinary adventures of this man, which he received from the lips of Colonel Boone himself. On one occasion, four Indians suddenly appeared before his cabin and took him prisoner. Though the delicacy of Colonel Boone's organization was such, that he could never himself relish tobacco in any form, he still raised some for his friends and neighbors, and for what were then deemed the essential rites of hospitality.

> "As a shelter for curing the tobacco, he had built an enclosure of rails a dozen feet in height and covered with canes and grass. Stalks of tobacco are generally split and strung on sticks about four feet in length. The ends of these are laid on poles placed across the tobacco house, and in tiers one above another, to the roof. Boone had fixed his temporary shelter in such a manner as to have three tiers. He had covered the lower tier and the tobacco had become dry; when he entered the shelter for the purpose of removing the sticks to the upper tier, preparatory to gathering the

British Allies

remainder of the crop. He had hoisted up the sticks from the lower to the second tier, and was standing on the poles which supported it, while raising the sticks to the upper tier, when four stout Indians, with guns, entered the low door and called him by name.

"'Now, Boone, we got you. You no get away more. We carry you off to Chilicothe this time. You no cheat us anymore.'

"Boone looked down upon their upturned faces, saw their loaded guns pointed at his breast, and recognising some of his old friends the Shawanese, who had made him prisoner near the Blue Licks in 1778, coolly and pleasantly responded:

"'Ah, old friends, glad to see you.'

"Perceiving that they manifested impatience to have him come down, he told them he was quite willing to go with them, and only begged that they would wait where they were, and watch him closely until he could finish removing the tobacco.

"While thus parleying with them, Boone inquired earnestly respecting his old friends in Chilicothe. He continued for some time to divert the attention of these simple-minded men, by allusions to past events with which they were familiar, and by talking of his tobacco, his mode of curing it, and promising them an abundant supply. With their guns in their hands however, they stood at the door of the shed, grouped closely together so as to render his escape apparently impossible. In the meantime Boone carefully gathered his arms full of the long, dry tobacco leaves, filled with pungent dust, which would be blinding and stifling as the most powerful snuff, and then with a leap from his station twelve feet high, came directly upon their heads, filling their eyes and nostrils, and so bewildering and disabling them for the moment, that they lost all self-possession and all self-control.

"Boone, agile as a deer, darted out at the door, and in a moment was in his bullet-proof log-hut, which to him was an impregnable citadel. Loop-holes guarded every approach. The Indians could not show themselves without exposure to certain death. They were too well acquainted with the unerring aim of Boone's rifle to venture within its range. Keeping the log cabin between them and their redoubtable foe, the baffled Indians fled into the wilderness.

"Colonel Boone related this adventure with great glee, imitating the gestures of the bewildered Indians. He said that notwithstanding his narrow escape, he could not resist the temptation, as he reached the door of his cabin, to look around to witness the effect of his achievement. The Indians coughing, sneezing, blinded and almost suffocated by the tobacco dust, were throwing out their arms and groping about in all directions, cursing him for a rogue and calling themselves fools."

Chapter 11

KENTUCKY ORGANIZED AS A STATE

The close of the war of the Revolution, bringing peace between the colonies and the mother country, deprived the Indians of that powerful alliance which had made them truly formidable. Being no longer able to obtain a supply of ammunition from the British arsenals, or to be guided in their murderous raids by British intelligence, they also, through their chiefs, entered into treaties of peace with the rapidly-increasing emigrants.

Though these treaties with the Indians prevented any general organization of the tribes, vagabond Indians, entirely lawless, were wandering in all directions, ever ready to perpetrate any outrage. Civil society has its highway robbers, burglars and murderers. Much more so was this the case among these savages, exasperated by many wrongs; for it cannot be denied that they were more frequently sinned against than sinning. Their untutored natures made but little distinction between the innocent and the guilty. If a vagabond white man wantonly shot an Indian—and many were as ready to do it as to shoot a wolf—the friends of the murdered Indian would take revenge upon the inmates of the first white man's cabin they encountered in the wilderness. Thus it was necessary for the pioneers to be constantly upon their guard. If they wandered any distance from the fort while hunting, or were hoeing in the field, or ventured to rear a cabin on a fertile meadow at a distance from the stations, they were liable to be startled at any hour of the day or of the night by the terrible war-whoop, and to feel the weight of savage vengeance.

This exposure to constant peril influenced the settlers, as a general rule, to establish themselves in stations. This gave them companionship, the benefits of co-operative labor, and security against any small prowling bands. These stations were formed upon the model of the one which Daniel Boone had so wisely organized at Boonesborough. They consisted of a cluster of bullet-proof log-cabins, arranged in a quadrangular form, so as to enclose a large internal area. All the doors opened upon this interior space. Here the cattle were gathered at night. The intervals between the cottages were filled with palisades, also bullet-proof. Loop-holes through the logs enabled these riflemen to guard every approach to their fortress. Thus they had little to fear from the Indians when sheltered by these strong citadels.

Emigration to Kentucky began very rapidly to increase. Large numbers crossed the mountains to Pittsburgh, where they took flat boats and floated down the beautiful Ohio, *la belle rivière*, until they reached such points on its southern banks as pleased them for a settlement, or from which they could ascend the majestic rivers of that peerless State. Comfortable homesteads were fast rising in all directions. Horses, cattle, swine, and poultry of all kinds were multiplied. Farming utensils began to make their appearance. The hum of happy industry was heard where wolves had formerly howled and buffalo ranged. Merchandise in considerable quantities was transported over the mountains on pack horses, and then floated down the Ohio and distributed among the settlements upon its banks. Country stores arose, land speculators appeared, and continental paper money became a circulating medium. This money, however, was not of any very great value, as may be inferred from the following decree, passed by one of the County Courts, establishing the schedule of prices for tavern-keeping:

"The Court doth set the following rates to be observed by keepers in this county: Whiskey, fifteen dollars the half-pint; rum, ten dollars the gallon; a meal, twelve dollars; stabling or pasturage, four dollars the night."

Kentucky Organized as a State

Under these changed circumstances, Colonel Boone, whose intrepidity nothing could daunt, and whose confidence in the protective power of his rifle was unbounded, had reared for himself, on one of the beautiful meadows of the Kentucky, a commodious home. He had selected a spot whose fertility and loveliness pleased his artistic eye.

It is estimated that during the years 1783 and 1784 nearly twelve thousand persons emigrated to Kentucky. Still all these had to move with great caution, with rifles always loaded, and ever on the alert against surprise. The following incident will give the reader an idea of the perils and wild adventures encountered by these parties in their search for new and distant homes.

Colonel Thomas Marshall, a man of much note in those days, had crossed the Alleghanies with his large family. At Pittsburgh he purchased a flat-boat, and was floating down the Ohio. He had passed the mouth of the Kanawha River without any incident of note occurring. About ten o'clock one night, as his boat had drifted near the northern shore of the solitary stream, he was hailed by a man upon the bank, who, after inquiring who he was, where he was bound, etc., added:

> "I have been posted here by order of my brother, Simon Gerty, to warn all boats of the danger of permitting themselves to be decoyed ashore. My brother regrets very deeply the injury he has inflicted upon the white men, and to convince them of the sincerity of his repentance, and of his earnest desire to be restored to their society, he has stationed me here to warn all boats of the snares which are spread for them by the cunning of the Indians. Renegade white men will be placed upon the banks, who will represent themselves as in the greatest distress. Even children taken captive will be compelled, by threats of torture, to declare that they are all alone upon the shore, and to entreat the boats to come and rescue them.
>
> "But keep in the middle of the river," said Gerty, "and steel your heart against any supplications you may hear."

The Colonel thanked him for his warning, and continued to float down the rapid current of the stream.

Virginia had passed a law establishing the town of Louisville, at the Falls of the Ohio. A very thriving settlement soon sprang up there.

The nature of the warfare still continuing between the whites and the Indians may be inferred from the following narrative, which we give in the words of Colonel Boone:

> "The Indians continued to practice mischief secretly upon the inhabitants in the exposed part of the country. In October a party made an incursion into a district called Crab Orchard. One of these Indians having advanced some distance before the others, boldly entered the house of a poor defenseless family, in which was only a negro man, a woman and her children, terrified with apprehensions of immediate death. The savage, perceiving their defenseless condition, without offering violence to the family, attempted to capture the negro, who happily proved an over-match for him, and threw the Indian on the ground.
>
> "In the struggle, the mother of the children drew an axe from the corner of the cottage and cut off the head of the Indian, while her little daughter shut the door. The savages soon appeared, and applied their tomahawks to the door. An old rusty gun-barrel, without a lock, lay in the corner, which the mother put through a small crevice, and the savages perceiving it, fled. In the meantime the alarm spread through the neighborhood; the armed men collected immediately and pursued the savages into the wilderness. Thus Providence, by means of this negro, saved the whole of the poor family from destruction."

The heroism of Mrs. Merrill is worthy of being perpetuated, not only as a wonderful achievement, but as illustrative of the nature of this dreadful warfare. Mr. Merrill, with his wife, little son and daughter, occupied a remote cabin in Nelson County, Kentucky. On the 24th of December, 1791, he was alarmed by the barking of his dog. Opening the door to ascertain the cause, he was instantly fired upon by seven or eight Indians who had crept near the house secreting themselves behind stumps and trees. Two bullets struck him, fracturing the bones both of his leg and of his arm. The savages, with hideous yells, then rushed for the door.

Mrs. Merrill had but just time to close and bolt it when the savages plunged against it and hewed it with their tomahawks. Every dwelling was at that time a fortress whose log walls were bullet proof. But for the terrible wounds which Mr. Merrill had received, he would with his rifle shooting through loop-holes, soon have put the savages to flight. They, emboldened by the supposition that he was killed, cut away at the door till they had opened a hole sufficiently large to crawl through. One of the savages attempted to enter. He had got nearly in when Mrs. Merrill cleft his skull with an ax, and he fell lifeless upon the floor. Another, supposing that he had safely effected an entrance, followed him and encountered the same fate. Four more of the savages were in this way despatched, when the others, suspecting that all was not right, climbed upon the roof and two of them endeavored to descend through the chimney. The noise they made directed the attention of the inmates of the cabin to the new danger.

There was a gentle fire burning upon the hearth. Mr. Merrill, with much presence of mind, directed his son, while his wife guarded the opening of the door with her ax, to empty the contents of a feather bed upon the fire. The dense smothering smoke filled the flue of the chimney. The two savages, suffocated with the fumes, after a few convulsive efforts to ascend fell almost insensible down upon the hearth. Mr. Merrill, seizing with his unbroken arm a billet of wood, despatched them both. But one of the Indians now remained. Peering in at the opening in the door he received a blow from the ax of Mrs. Merrill which severely wounded him. Bleeding and disheartened he fled alone into the wilderness, the only one of the eight who survived the conflict.

A white man who was at that time a prisoner among the Indians and who subsequently effected his escape, reported that when the wounded savage reached his tribe he said to the white captive in broken English:

> "I have bad news for the poor Indian. Me lose a son, me lose a broder. The squaws have taken the breech clout, and fight worse than the long knives."

But the Indians were not always the aggressors. Indeed it is doubtful whether they would ever have raised the war-whoop against the white man, had it not been for the outrages they were so constantly experiencing from unprincipled and vagabond adventurers, who were ever infesting the frontiers. The following incident illustrates the character and conduct of these miscreants:

A party of Indian hunters from the South wandering through their ancient hunting grounds of Kentucky, accidentally came upon a settlement where they found several horses grazing in the field. They stole the horses, and commenced a rapid retreat to their own country. Three young men, Davis, Caffre and McClure, pursued them. Not being able to overtake the fugitives, they decided to make reprisals on the first Indians they should encounter. It so happened that they soon met three Indian hunters. The parties saluted each other in a friendly manner, and proceeded on their way in pleasant companionship.

The young men said that they observed the Indians conversing with one another in low tones of voice, and thus they became convinced that the savages meditated treachery. Resolving to anticipate the Indians' attack, they formed the following plan. While walking together in friendly conversation, the Indians being entirely off their guard, Caffre, who was a very powerful man, was to spring upon the lightest of the Indians, crush him to the ground, and thus take him a prisoner. At the same instant, Davis and McClure were each to shoot one of the other Indians, who, being thus taken by surprise, could offer no resistance.

The signal was given. Caffre sprang upon his victim and bore him to the ground. McClure shot his man dead. Davis' gun flashed in the pan. The Indian thus narrowly escaping death immediately aimed his gun at Caffre, who was struggling with the one he had grappled, and instantly killed him. McClure in his turn shot the Indian. There was now one Indian and two white men. But the Indian had the loaded rifle. McClure's was discharged and Davis' missed fire. The Indian, springing from the grasp of his dying antagonist, presented his rifle at Davis, who immediately fled, hotly pursued by the Indian. McClure, stopping only to reload his gun, followed after them. Soon he lost sight of both. Davis was never heard of afterwards. Doubtless he was shot by the avenging Indian, who returned to his wigwam with the white man's scalp.

McClure, after this bloody fray, being left alone in the wilderness, commenced a return to his distant home. He had not proceeded far before he met an Indian on horseback accompanied by a boy on foot. The warrior dismounted, and in token of peace offered McClure his pipe. As they were seated together upon a log, conversing, McClure said that the Indian informed him by signs that there were other Indians in the distance who would soon come up, and that then they should take him captive, tie his feet beneath the horse's belly and carry him off to their village. McClure seized his gun, shot the Indian through the heart, and plunging into the forest, effected his escape.

About this same time Captain James Ward, with a party of half a dozen white men, one of whom was his nephew, and a number of horses, was floating down the Ohio River from Pittsburgh. They were in a flat boat about forty-five feet long and eight feet wide. The gunwale of the boat consisted of but a single pine plank. It was beautiful weather, and for several days they were swept along by the tranquil stream, now borne by the changing current towards the one shore, and now towards the other. One morning when they had been swept by the stream within about one hundred and fifty feet of the northern shore, suddenly several hundred Indians appeared upon the bank, and uttering savage yells opened upon them a terrible fire.

Captain Ward's nephew, pierced by a ball in the breast, fell dead in the bottom of the boat. Every horse was struck by a bullet. Some were instantly killed; others, severely wounded, struggled so violently as to cause the frail bark to dip water, threatening immediate destruction. All the crew except Captain Ward were so panic-stricken by this sudden assault, that they threw themselves flat upon their faces in the bottom of the boat, and attempted no resistance where even the exposure of a hand would be the target for a hundred rifles.

Fortunately Captain Ward was protected from this shower of bullets by a post, which for some purpose had been fastened to the gunwale. He therefore retained his position at the helm, which was an oar, striving to guide the boat to the other side of the river. As the assailants had no canoes, they could not attempt to board, but for more than an hour they ran along the banks yelling and keeping up an almost constant fire. At length the boat was swept to the other side of the stream, when the miscreants abandoned the pursuit, and disappeared.

Quite a large party of emigrants were attacked by the Indians near what is now called Scagg's Creek, and six were instantly killed. A Mrs. McClure, delirious with terror, fled she knew not where, followed by her three little children and carrying a little babe in her arms. The cries of the babe guided the pursuit of the Indians. They cruelly tomahawked the three oldest children, and took the mother and the babe as captives. Fortunately the tidings of this outrage speedily reached one of the settlements. Captain Whitley immediately started in pursuit of the gang. He overtook them, killed two, wounded two, and rescued the captives. Such were the scenes enacted during a period of nominal peace with the Indians.

There has been transmitted to us a very curious document, giving an account of a speech made by Mr. Dalton, a Government agent, to a council of Indian chiefs, upon the announcement of peace with Great Britain, and their reply. Mr. Dalton said:

> "My Children,—What I have often told you is now come to pass. This day I received news from my great chief at the Falls of the Ohio. Peace is made with the enemies of America. The white flesh, the Americans, French, and Spanish, this day smoked out of the peace-pipe. The tomahawk is buried, and they are now friends. I am told the Shawanese, the Delawares, Chickasaws, Cherokees, and all other red flesh, have taken the Long Knife by the hand. They have given up to them the prisoners that were in their hands.
>
> "My children on the Wabash, open your ears and let what I tell you sink into your hearts. You know me. Near twenty years I have been among you. The Long Knife is my nation. I know their hearts. Peace they carry in one hand and war in the other. I leave you to yourselves to judge. Consider and now accept the one or the other. We never beg peace of our enemies. If you love your women and children, receive the belt of wampum I present you. Return me my flesh you have in your villages, and the horses you stole from my people in Kentucky. Your corn fields were never disturbed by the Long Knife. Your women and children lived

quiet in their houses, while your warriors were killing and robbing my people. All this you know is the truth.

"This is the last time I shall speak to you. I have waited six moons to hear you speak and to get my people from you. In ten nights I shall leave the Wabash to see my great chief at the Falls of the Ohio, where he will be glad to hear from your own lips what you have to say. Here is tobacco I give you. Smoke and consider what I have said."

Mr. Dalton then presented Piankashaw, the chief of the leading tribe assembled in council, with a belt of blue and white wampum. Piankashaw received the emblem of peace with much dignity, and replied:

"My Great Father the Long Knife,—You have been many years among us. You have suffered by us. We still hope you will have pity and compassion upon us, on our women and children. The sun shines on us, and the good news of peace appears in our faces. This is the day of joy to the Wabash Indians. With one tongue we now speak. We accept your peace-belt.

"We received the tomahawk from the English. Poverty forced us to it. We were followed by other tribes. We are sorry for it. To-day we collect the scattered bones of our friends and bury them in one grave. We thus plant the tree of peace, that God may spread its branches so that we can all be secured from bad weather. Here is the pipe that gives us joy. Smoke out of it. Our warriors are glad you are the man we present it to. We have buried the tomahawk, have formed friendship never to be broken, and now we smoke out of your pipe.

"My father, we know that the Great Spirit was angry with us for stealing your horses and attacking your people. He has sent us so much snow and cold weather as to kill your horses with our own. We are a poor people. We hope God will help us, and that the Long Knife will have compassion on our women and children. Your people who are with us are well. We shall collect them when they come in from hunting. All the prisoners taken in Kentucky are alive. We love them, and so do our young women. Some of your people mend our guns, and others tell us they can make rum out of corn. They are now the same as we. In one moon after this we will take them back to their friends in Kentucky.

"My father, this being the day of joy to the Wabash Indians, we beg a little drop of your milk to let our warriors see that it came from your own breast. We were born and raised in the woods. We could never learn to make rum. God has made the white men masters of the world."

Having finished his speech, Piankashaw presented Mr. Dalton with three strings of blue and white wampum as the seal of peace. All must observe the strain of despondency which pervades this address, and it is melancholy to notice the imploring tones with which the chief asks for rum, the greatest curse which ever afflicted his people.

The incessant petty warfare waged between vagrant bands of the whites and the Indians, with the outrages perpetrated on either side, created great exasperation. In the year 1784 there were many indications that the Indians were again about to combine in an attack upon the settlements. These stations were widely scattered, greatly exposed, and there were many of them. It was impossible for the pioneers to rally in sufficient strength to protect every position. The savages, emerging unexpectedly from the wilderness, could select their own point of attack, and could thus cause a vast amount of loss and misery. For a long time it had been unsafe for any individual, or even small parties, unless very thoroughly armed, to wander beyond the protection of the forts. Under these circumstances, a convention was held of the leading men of Kentucky at the Danville Station, to decide what measures to adopt in view of the threatened invasion. It was quite certain that the movement of the savages would be so sudden and impetuous that the settlers would be compelled to rely mainly upon their own resources.

The great State of Virginia, of which Kentucky was but a frontier portion, had become rich and powerful. But many weary leagues intervened, leading through forests and over craggy mountains, between the plains of these distant counties and Richmond, the capital of Virginia. The convention at Danville discussed the question whether it were not safer for them to anticipate the Indians, and immediately to send an army for the destruction of their towns and crops north of the Ohio. But here they were embarrassed by the consideration that they had no legal power to make this movement, and that the whole question, momentous as it was and demanding immediate action, must be referred to the State Government, far away beyond the mountains. This involved long delay, and it could hardly be expected that the members of the General Court in their peaceful homes would fully sympathize with the unprotected settlers in their exposure to the tomahawk and the scalping knife.

Several conventions were held, and the question was earnestly discussed whether the interests of Kentucky did not require her separation from the Government of Virginia, and her organization as a self-governing State. The men who had boldly ventured to seek new homes so far beyond the limits of civilization were generally men of great force of character and of political foresight. They had just emerged from the war of the Revolution, during which all the most important questions of civil polity had been thoroughly canvassed. Their meetings were conducted with great dignity and calm deliberation.

On the twenty-third of May, 1785, the convention at Danville passed the resolve with great unanimity that Kentucky ought to be separated from Virginia, and received into the American Union, upon the same basis as the other States. Still that they might not act upon a question of so much importance without due deliberation, they referred the subject to another convention to be assembled at Danville in August. This convention reiterated the resolution of its predecessor; issued a proclamation urging the people everywhere to organise for defence against the Indians, and appointed a delegation of two members to proceed to Richmond, and present their request for a separation to the authorities there.

"The Legislature of Virginia was composed of men too wise not to see that separation was inevitable. Separated from the parent State by distance and by difficulties of communication, in those days most formidable, they saw that Kentuckians would not long submit to be ruled by those whose power was so far removed as to surround every approach to it with the greatest embarrassment. It was, without its wrongs, and tyranny and misgovernment, the repetition of the circumstances of the Crown and Colonies; and with good judgment, and as the beautiful language of the Danville convention expressed it, with sole intent to bless its people, they agreed to a dismemberment of its part, to secure the happiness of the whole."[6]

It is not important here to enter into a detail of the various discussions which ensued, and of the measures which were adopted. It is sufficient to say that the communication from Kentucky to the Legislature of Virginia was referred to the illustrious John Marshall, then at the commencement of his distinguished career. He gave to the request of the petitioners his own strong advocacy. The result was, that a decree was passed after tedious delays, authorising the formal separation of Kentucky from Virginia. On the fourth of February, 1791, the new State, by earnest recommendation of George Washington, was admitted into the American Union.

It does not appear that Colonel Boone was a member of any of these conventions. He had no taste for the struggles in political assemblies. He dreaded indeed the speculator, the land jobber, and the intricate decisions of courts, more than the tomahawk of the Indian. And he knew full well that should the hour of action come, he would be one of the first to be summoned to the field. While therefore others of the early pioneers were engaged in these important deliberations, he was quietly pursuing those occupations, congenial to his tastes, of cultivating the farm, or in hunting game in the solitude of the forests. His humble cabin stood upon the banks of the Kentucky River, not far from the station at Boonesborough. And thoroughly acquainted as he was with the habits of the Indians, he felt quite able, in his bullet-proof citadel, to protect himself from any marauding bands which might venture to show themselves so near the fort.

It seems to be the lot of humanity that life should be composed of a series of storms, rising one after another. In the palace and in the cottage, in ancient days and at the present time, we find the sweep of the inexorable law, that man is born to mourn.

"Sorrow is for the sons of men,
And weeping for earth's daughters."

---

[6] Daniel Boone, by W. H. Bogart.

Kentucky Organized as a State

The cloud of menaced Indian invasion had passed away, when suddenly the sheriff appears in Boone's little cabin, and informs him that his title to his land is disputed, and that legal proceedings were commenced against him. Boone could not comprehend this. Kentucky he regarded almost his own by the right of his discovery. He had led the way there. He had established himself and family in the land, and had defended it from the incursions of the Indians. And now, in his advancing years, to be driven from the few acres he had selected and to which he supposed he had a perfect title, seemed to him very unjust indeed. He could not recognise any right in what seemed to him but the quibbles of the lawyers. In his autobiography he wrote in reference to his many painful adventures:

"My footsteps have often been marked with blood. Two darling sons and a brother have I lost by savage hands, which have also taken from me forty valuable horses and abundance of cattle. Many dark and sleepless nights have I been a companion for owls, separated from the cheerful society of men, scorched by the summer's sun, and pinched by the winter's cold, an instrument ordained to settle the wilderness."

Agitated by the thought of the loss of his farm and deeply wounded in his feelings, as though a great wrong had been inflicted upon him, Boone addressed an earnest memorial to the Legislature of Kentucky. In this he stated that immediately after the troubles with the Indians had ceased, he located himself upon lands to which he supposed he had a perfect title; that he reared his house and commenced cultivating his fields. And after briefly enumerating the sacrifices he had made in exploring, settling and defending Kentucky, he said he could not understand the justice of making a set of complicated forms of law, superior to his actual occupancy of the land selected, as he believed when and where it was, it was his unquestioned right to do so.

But the lawyers and the land speculators were too shrewd for the pioneer. Colonel Boone was sued; the question went to the courts which he detested, and Boone lost his farm. It was indeed a very hard case. He had penetrated the country when no other white man trod its soil. He discovered its wonderful resources, and proclaimed them to the world. He had guided settlers into the region, and by his sagacity and courage, had provided for their wants and protected them from the savage. And now in his declining years he found himself driven from his farm, robbed of every acre, a houseless, homeless, impoverished man. The deed was so cruel that thousands since, in reading the recital, have been agitated by the strongest emotions of indignation and grief.

Chapter 12

ADVENTURES ROMANTIC AND PERILOUS

The Indians still continued hostile. The following incident gives one an idea of the nature of the conflict which continued, and of the perils which were encountered.

There was a striving station where a few settlers were collected, at a spot now called State Creek Iron Works. One or two farm-houses were scattered around, but at such a short distance from the fort that their inmates could at once take refuge behind its log walls, in case of alarm. In the month of August, 1786, a young man residing in the fort, by the name of Yates, called at one of these farm-houses and requested a lad, Francis Downing, to accompany him in search of a horse, which had strayed away. The two friends set out together, and after searching the forest in vain, found themselves, the latter part of the afternoon, in a lonely uninhabited valley, nearly seven miles from the fort. Here young Downing became quite alarmed by some indications that Indians were dogging their steps. He communicated his fears to his companion. But Yates, who was several years older than Downing, was an experienced hunter and inured to life in the woods, had become to a certain degree indifferent to danger. He made himself quite merry over his young companion's fears, asking him at what price he was willing to sell his scalp, and offering to insure it for sixpence.

Still Downing was not satisfied, and his alarm increased as he insisted that he occasionally heard the crack of dry twigs behind them, as if broken by some one pursueing. But Yates deriding his fears, pressed on, making the woods resound with a song, to which he gave utterance from unusually full and strong lungs. Downing gradually slackened his pace, and when Yates was some thirty yards in advance of him, sprang into a dense cluster of tall whortleberry bushes, where he was effectually concealed. Scarcely had he done this, when to his great terror he saw two Indians peeping cautiously out of a thick canebrake. Deceived by the song of Yates, who with stentorian lungs was still giving forth his woodland ditty, they supposed both had passed. Young Downing thought it impossible but that the savages must have seen him as he concealed himself. Greatly alarmed he raised his gun, intending to shoot one and to trust to his heels for escape from the other.

But his hand was so unsteady that the gun went off before he had taken aim. Terror stricken, he rushed along the path Yates had trod. Yates, alarmed by the report of the gun, came running back. As they met, the two Indians were seen not far from them in hot pursuit. They soon could easily see that the enemy was gaining upon them. In their rapid flight they came to a deep gulley which Yates cleared at a bound, but young Downing failed in the attempt. His breast struck the opposite almost precipitous bank, and he rolled to the bottom of the ditch. Some obstruction in the way prevented the Indians from witnessing the fall of Downing. They continued the pursuit of Yates, crossing the gulley a few yards below where Downing had met his mishap. Thus in less time than we have occupied in the narration, the Indians disappeared in their chase after Yates.

Downing was in great perplexity. He did not dare to creep out of the gulley, lest he should be seen, and as soon as the Indians should perceive that he was not with Yates, as they inevitably would ere long do, they would know that he was left behind, and would turn back for his capture. Unfortunately young Downing had so far lost his presence of mind, that he had failed to reload his gun. Just then he saw one of the savages returning, evidently in search of him. There was no possible resource left but flight. Throwing away his now useless gun, he rushed into the forest with all the speed which terror could inspire. He was but a boy, the full-grown Indian gained rapidly upon him, he could almost strike him with his tomahawk, when they came to an immense tree, blown up by the roots. The boy ran on one side of the trunk and the Indian on the other, towards the immense pile of earth which adhered to the upturned roots.

The boy now gave up all hope in utter despair. It seemed certain that the brawny Indian would get ahead of him and intercept his further flight. But it so happened—was it an accident or was it a Providence—that a she-bear had made her bed directly in the path which the Indian with almost blind eagerness was pursuing. Here the ferocious beast was suckling her cubs. The bear sprang from her lair, and instantly with a terrific hug grasped the savage in her paws. The Indian gave a terrific yell and plunged his knife again and again into the body of the bear. The boy had but one brief glance, as in this bloody embrace they rolled over and over on the ground. The boy, praying that the bear might tear the Indian in pieces, added new speed to his flight and reached the fort in safety.

There he found Yates who had arrived but a few moments before him, and who had outrun the other Indian. The next morning a well-armed party returned to the tree. Both the bear and the Indian had disappeared. Probably both had suffered very severely in the conflict, and both had escaped with their lives.

Another incident illustrative of these perilous adventures in the now peaceful State of Kentucky. Mr. Rowan, with his own and five other families, left the little hamlet at Louisville to float down the Ohio to Green River, and to ascend that stream, intending to rear their new homes on its fertile and delightful banks. The families were quite comfortably accommodated in a large flat-bottomed boat. Another boat of similar construction conveyed their cattle and sundry articles of household furniture. On the route which they were pursuing, there were then no settlements. The Ohio River and the Green river flowed through unbroken solitudes.

The flat boats had floated down the beautiful Ohio, through scenes of surpassing loveliness, about one hundred miles, when one night about ten o'clock a prodigious shouting and yelling of Indians was heard some distance farther down the river on the northern shore. Very soon they came in sight of their camp-fires, which were burning very brightly. It was evident that the Indians were having a great carousal rejoicing over some victory. Mr. Rowan immediately ordered the two boats to be lashed firmly together. There were but seven men on board who were capable of making efficient use of the rifle. Plying the oars as vigorously and noiselessly as they could, they endeavored to keep close to the Kentucky shore. And yet they were careful not to approach too near, lest there might be Indians there also. It was evident that there was a large gathering of the Indians on the northern bank, for their camp-fires extended for a distance of nearly half a mile along the river.

As the boats floated noiselessly along in the gloom of the night, under shadow of the cliffs, they were not detected until they were opposite the central fire, whose brilliancy threw a flood of light nearly across the stream. A simultaneous shout greeted this discovery, and with terrific yells the savages rushed to their canoes and commenced a pursuit. The two flat boats rapidly floated beyond the illumination of the fires into the region of midnight darkness. The timid Indians, well acquainted with the white man's unerring aim, pursued cautiously, though their hideous yells resounded along the shores.

Mr. Rowan ordered all on board to keep perfect silence, to conceal themselves as much as possible, and ordered not a gun to be fired till the Indians were so near that the powder of the gun would burn them, thus rendering every shot absolutely certain. The Indians, with their hideous yells, pursued in their canoes until within a hundred yards of the boats. They then seemed simultaneously to have adopted the conviction that the better part of valor was discretion. In the darkness, they could not see the boatmen, who they had no doubt were concealed behind bullet-proof bulwarks. Their birch canoes presented not the slightest obstruction to the passage of a rifle ball. Knowing that the flash of a gun from the boat would be certain death to some one of their number, and that thus the boatmen, with the rapidity with which they could load and fire, would destroy a large part of their company before they could hope to capture the flat boats, they hesitated to approach any nearer, but followed in the pursuit for nearly three miles down the river, assailing the white men only with harmless yells.

The heroic Mrs. Rowan, as she saw the canoes approaching, supposing that the savages would attempt to board the boats, crept quietly around in the darkness, collected all the axes, and placed one by the side of each man, leaning the handle against his knee. While performing this significant act she uttered not a word, but returned to her own seat in silence, retaining a sharp hatchet for herself.

With such determined spirits to assail, it was well for the savages that they did not approach within arms-length of those whom they were pursuing. They would certainly have met with a bloody reception.

The savages at length, despairing of success, relinquished the pursuit and returned to their demoniac orgies around their camp-fires. It was supposed that they had captured a boat which was descending the river the day before, and that their extraordinary revelry was accompanied by the roasting of their captives. A son of Mr. Rowan, but ten years of age, who subsequently became one of the most distinguished men in Kentucky, was present on this occasion. He frequently, in after-years, alluded to the indescribable sensations of sublimity and terror which the scene inspired. The gloom of the night; the solemn flow of the majestic river; the dim view of the forests on either side; the gleam of the camp-fires of the Indians, around which the half-clad savages were dancing in hideous contortions; the unearthly yells in which every demoniac passion seemed contending for the mastery; the shout which was given when they discovered the boats beneath the shadows of the opposite cliffs; the pursuit of the canoes with redoubled vehemence of hooting; the rapidity with which, with brawny arms, they paddled their boats to and fro; the breathless silence which pervaded the flat boat while for more than an hour the occupants awaited, momentarily expecting the terrible onset; and above all, the fortitude and heroism displayed by his mother,—all these combined to leave an impression upon the mind of the boy which could never be obliterated. Few will be able to read the record of this adventure without emotion. What then must it have been to have experienced it in bodily presence, and to have shared in all its terrible dangers?

As we have before said, there was no distinctly proclaimed war, at this time, between the pioneers and the Indians. While lawless men on both sides were committing the most atrocious outrages, the chiefs and the legitimate authorities were nominally at peace. The red men, whether engaged in what they deemed lawful warfare, or moving in plundering bands, were in the habit of inflicting upon their captives the most dreadful tortures which their ingenuity could devise. The white men could not retaliate by the perpetration of such revolting cruelty.

It probably was a suggestion of Colonel Boone that a council might be held with the Indian chiefs, and a treaty formed by which prisoners should be exempted from torture and exchanged, as in civilized warfare. The Indians were by no means reckless of the lives of their warriors, and would probably be very ready to give up a white captive if by so doing they could receive one of their own braves in return. A council was held at a station where Maysville now stands. Colonel Boone was at once selected as the man of all others most fit to take part in these deliberations. He was not only thoroughly acquainted with the Indians, their habits, their modes of thought, and the motives most likely to influence their minds; but his own peculiar character seemed just the one calculated to inspire them with admiration.

The principle was here adopted of an exchange of prisoners, which notwithstanding the continued violence of the lawless, saved the lives of many captives. It is an interesting fact, illustrative of the sagacity and extraordinary power of Colonel Boone over the Indian mind, that the chiefs with one consent agreed in grateful commemoration of this treaty, that if any captive should hereafter be taken by them from Maysville, that captive should be treated with every possible degree of lenity. And it is worthy of record that such a captive was subsequently taken, and that the Indians with the most scrupulous fidelity fulfilled their pledge. Indeed, it is difficult for an impartial historian to deny, that these poor savages, ignorant and cruel as they were, often displayed a sense of honor which we do not so often find in their opponents. It is to be feared that were Indian historians to write the record of these wars, we should not find that they were always in the wrong.

Colonel Boone, ejected from his lands and thus left penniless, felt keenly the wrongs which were inflicted upon him. He knew full well that he had done a thousand times more for Kentucky than any other man living or dead. He had conferred upon the State services which no money could purchase. Though to his intimate friends he confided his sufferings, he was too proud to utter loud complaints. In silence he endured. But Kentucky had ceased to be a happy home for him. Over all its broad and beautiful expanse which he had opened to the world, there was not a single acre which he could call his own. And he had no money with which to purchase a farm of those speculators, into whose hands most of the lands had fallen. Could the good old man now rise from his grave, a Kentucky Legislature would not long leave him landless. There is scarcely a cabin or a mansion in the whole State, where Daniel Boone would not meet with as hospitable a reception as grateful hearts could give.

As a grief-stricken child rushes to its mother's arms for solace, so it is natural for man, when world-weary and struggling with adversity, to look back with longing eyes to the home of his childhood. The remembrance of its sunny days animates him, and its trivial sadnesses are forgotten. Thus with Daniel Boone; houseless and stung by ingratitude, he turned his eyes to the far distant home of his childhood, on the banks of the Schuykill. More than forty years of a wonderfully adventurous life had passed, since he a boy of fourteen had accompanied his father in his removal from Reading, in Berk's County, to North Carolina. Still the remarkable boy had left traces behind him which were not yet obliterated.

He visited Reading, probably influenced by a faint hope of finding there a home. A few of his former acquaintances were living, and many family friends remained. By all he was received with the greatest kindness. But the frontier settlement of log huts, and the majestic surrounding forests filled with game, had entirely disappeared. Highly cultivated farms, from which even the stumps of the forest had perished, extended in all directions. Ambitious mansions adorned the hillsides, and all the appliances of advancing civilization met the eye. There could be no home here for Daniel Boone. Amid these strange scenes he felt as a stranger, and his heart yearned again for the solitudes of the forest. He longed to get beyond the reach of lawyers' offices, and court-houses, and land speculators.

After a short visit he bade adieu forever to his friends upon the Schuykill, and turned his steps again towards the setting sun. His feelings had been too deeply wounded to allow him to think of remaining a man without a home in Kentucky. Still the idea of leaving a region endeared to him by so many memories must have been very painful. He remembered vividly his long and painful journeys over the mountains, through the wilderness untrodden by the foot of the white man; his solitary exploration of the new Eden which he seemed to have found there; the glowing accounts he had carried back to his friends of the sunny skies, the salubrious clime, the fertile soil, and the majesty and loveliness of the landscape; of mountain, valley, lake and river which Providence had lavished with a prodigal hand in this "Garden of the Lord."

One by one he had influenced his friends to emigrate, had led them to their new homes, had protected them against the savages, and now when Kentucky had become a prosperous State in the Union, containing thirty thousand inhabitants, he was cast aside, and under the forms of law was robbed of the few acres which he had cultivated as his own. His life embittered by these reflections, and seeing nothing to attract him in the wild and unknown regions beyond the Mississippi, Colonel Boone turned sadly back to Virginia.

It was an easy task for him to remove. In such an hour, one can sometimes well say, "Blessed be Nothing." A few pack-horses were sufficient to convey all his household goods. It is probable that his wife and children, indignant at the treatment which the husband and father had received, were glad to leave.

This was doubtless one of the saddest journeys that Colonel Boone ever undertook. Traversing an almost pathless wilderness in a direction a little north of east from Boonesborough, he crossed the various speers of the Alleghany range, supporting his family with his rifle on the way, until after passing over three hundred miles of the wilderness, he reached the mouth of the Kanawha river, as that stream flows from Virginia due north, and empties into the Ohio river. Here there was a point of land washed by the Ohio on the north, and the Great Kanawha on the west, to which the appropriate name of Point Pleasant had been given. It does not appear that civilization had as yet penetrated this region. The emigration to Kentucky had floated by it down the river, descending from Pittsburg, or had crossed the mountain passes from North Carolina, several hundred miles to the south.

Colonel Boone was now fifty-five years of age. If there were any settlement at the time at Point Pleasant, it must have consisted merely of a few log huts. Here at all events, Colonel Boone found the solitude and the communion with nature alone, for which his heart yearned. The world might call him poor, and still he was rich in the abundant supply of all his earthly wants. He reared his log hut where no one appeared to dispute his claim. The fertile soil around, a virgin soil, rich with undeveloped treasures, under the simplest culture produced abundantly, and the forest around supplied him daily with animal food more than a European peasant sees in a year.

Here Colonel Boone and his family remained for several years, to use a popular phrase, buried from the world. His life was mainly that of a hunter. Mr. Peck, speaking of the habits of those pioneers who depended mainly upon the rifle for support, writes:

> "I have often seen him get up early in the morning, walk hastily out, and look anxiously to the woods and snuff the autumnal winds with the highest rapture; then return into the house and cast a quick and attentive look at the rifle, which was always suspended to a joist by a couple of buck-horns or little forks. The hunting dog understanding the intentions of his master, would wag his tail, and by every blandishment in his power, express his readiness to accompany him to the woods."

It probably did not diminish Colonel Boone's interest in his new home, that it was exposed to all the perils of border life; that his rifle should be ever loaded; that his faithful watch-dog should be stationed at the door, to give warning of any approaching footsteps; and that he and his family should always be ready for a siege or battle. With these precautions, Boone had no more fear of assault from half a dozen vagabond Indians, than he had from so many howling wolves.

The casualties of life had greatly reduced his family. Of his three sons, the eldest had fallen beneath the arrow and the tomahawk of the savages amidst the gloomy defiles of the Alleghany Mountains. His second son was killed at the dreadful battle of the Blue Licks, as his agonised father had been compelled to abandon him to the merciless foe. His third son, probably chagrined by the treatment which his father had received from the authorities of Kentucky, had bidden adieu to all the haunts of civilized life, and traversing the wilderness towards the setting sun for many hundred miles, had crossed the Mississippi and sought a home in the wilds of the upper Louisiana, then under the dominion of Spain.

As Boone was quietly engaged in his solitary vocation of farmer and hunter, where there were no books, no newspapers, nothing whatever to inform him of what was transpiring in the busy world of civilization, or in the haunts of savage life, two or three hunters came one day to his cabin, where of course they met with a very hospitable reception. It was not difficult to entertain guests in those days. The floor of the cabin supplied all the needed accommodations for lodging. Each guest with his rifle could easily furnish more food than was desired for the whole family.

A little corn-meal, very coarsely ground in what was called a tub-mill, gave quite a variety of palatable food. Boiled in water it formed a dish called mush, which when eaten with milk, honey or butter, presented truly a delicious repast for hungry mouths. Mixed with cold water, it was ready to be baked. When covered with hot ashes, it emerged smoking from the glowing embers in the form of Ash Cake. When baked upon a shingle and placed before the coals, it was termed Journey Cake, so called because it could be so speedily prepared. This name has been corrupted in modern times into *Johnny* Cake. When baked upon a helveless hoe, it formed the Hoe Cake. When baked in a kettle covered with a heated lid, if in one large cake, it was called a Pone or loaf. If in quite a number of small cakes they were called Dodgers.

Corn flour seems to have been peculiarly prepared by Providence for the pioneers. For them it possesses some very great advantages over all other flour. It requires but few and the most simple cooking utensils. It can be rendered very palatable without either yeast, eggs, sugar or spices of any kind. It can easily be raised in the greatest abundance, and affords the most wholesome and nutritious food.

"Let pæans," writes Mr. Hartly, "be sung all over the mighty West, to Indian Corn. Without it, the West would still have been a wilderness. Was the frontier suddenly invaded, without commissary, or quartermaster, or other sources of supply, each soldier parched a peck of corn. A portion of it was put into his pockets, the remainder in his wallet, and throwing it upon his saddle with his rifle on his shoulder, he was ready in half an hour for the campaign. Did a flood of emigration inundate the frontier, with an amount of consumers disproportioned to the supply of grain, the facility of raising the Indian corn, and its early maturity, gave promise and guarantee that the scarcity would be temporary and tolerable. Did the safety of the frontier demand the services of every adult militiaman, the boys and women could themselves raise corn, and furnish ample supplies of bread. Did an autumnal intermittent confine the whole family, or the entire population to the sick bed, this certain concomitant of the clearing and cultivating the new soil, mercifully withholds its paroxysms till the crop of corn is made. It requires no further labor or care afterwards. Pæans, say we, and a temple of worshipping to the creator of Indian Corn!"

The hunters to whom we referred were indeed congenial companions to Daniel Boone. As day after day they accompanied him in the chase, and night after night sat by the blaze of his cabine-fire, related to him the adventures they had encountered far away beyond the Mississippi, the spirit of his youth revived within him. An irrepressible desire sprang up in his heart again to become a pioneer in the pathless forest which he loved so well. It is not improbable also that his parental feelings might have been aroused by the consideration that his son had gone before him to that distant land; and that he might have been animated by the hope of being reunited with him in his declining years.

The hunters represented to him that another Kentucky could be found beyond the Father of Waters; that the game was abundant and would be inexhaustible, until long after his earthly pilgrimage should end; that the

Spanish Government, desirous of promoting emigration, were ready to make the most liberal grants of land to any man who would rear a cabin and commence the cultivation of the soil; that over an expanse of hundreds of miles of a sunny clime, and as luxurious soil as heart could desire, he could select his broad acres with no fear of ever again being ejected from his home.

These representations were resistless. Colonel Boone decided again to become a wanderer to the far West, though it involved the relinquishment of American citizenship and becoming a subject of the crown of Spain.

The year 1795 had now come, as Colonel Boone gathered up his few household goods for the fourth great remove of his life. He was born on the banks of the Delaware; his childhood was passed amidst the solitudes of the Upper Skuylkill; his early manhood, where he reared his cabin and took to it his worthy bride, was in North Carolina. Thence penetrating the wilderness through adventures surpassing the dreams of romance, he had passed many years amidst the most wonderful vicissitudes of quietude and of agitation, of peace and of war, on the settlement of which he was the father, at Boonesborough, in the valley of the Kentucky River. Robbed of the possessions which he had earned a hundred times over, he had sought a temporary residence at Point Pleasant, in Virginia. And now, as he was approaching the termination of his three score years, he was prepared to traverse the whole extent of Kentucky, from the Alleghany border on the east, to the mighty flood of the Mississippi, which then upon the west rushed with its turbid flood through an almost unbroken solitude. It was a long, long journey.

We can only surmise the reasons why he did not float down the Ohio in a flat boat. It may be said that he was entirely unaccustomed to boating. And as it does not appear that any other families joined him in the enterprise, his solitary boat would be almost certain to be attacked and captured by some of the marauding bands which frequented the northern banks of the Ohio.

Colonel Boone was perfectly at home in the wilderness. He could always find a path for himself, where there was no trail to follow. And but few Indians now ventured into the interior of the State. We have no record of the journey. He reached the Mississippi safely, crossed the river into what is now the State of Missouri, and found a warm greeting in the cabin of his son Daniel M. Boone, who had established himself upon the western banks of the river, near where the city of St. Louis now stands.

Chapter 13

A NEW HOME

At the time when Colonel Boone crossed the Mississippi and entered Missouri, the Spanish Government, then in possession of that territory, being anxious to promote the settlement of the country, gave a very cordial welcome to all emigrants. The fame of Colonel Boone, as one of the most bold and valuable of pioneers, had preceded him. The Lieutenant Governor under the Spanish crown, who resided at St. Louis, received him with marked attention, and gave him the assurance that ample portions of land should be given to him and his family.

Colonel Boone took up his residence, with his son, in what is called the Femme Osage district. The Spanish authorities appointed him Commandant of the district, which was an office of both civil and military power. His commission was dated July 11th, 1800. Remote as was this region from the Atlantic States, bold adventurers, lured by the prospect of obtaining large tracts of land, were rapidly pouring in. Instead of collecting together, they scattered wildly over the vast domain. Don Charles, the Spanish governor, gave Colonel Boone eight thousand acres of land on the north side of the Missouri river. By the law of the province he was bound to build upon some part of this land a house within the year, and also to obtain a confirmation of the grant from the representative of the Spanish crown, then residing in New Orleans. Both of these precautions the simple-minded man neglected to adopt. To visit New Orleans required a journey through the wilderness of more than a thousand miles. Though he might float down the stream in his boat he would be exposed continually to attacks from the Indians on its banks, and when ready to return he could not surmount the rapid current of the river in his boat, but would be compelled to traverse the winding banks, often through almost impenetrable forests and morasses. His duties as *syndic* or justice of the peace also occupied much of his time, and the Lieutenant Governor at St. Louis agreed to dispense with his residence upon his lands. In addition to this, Colonel Boone had no doubt that the country would soon come under the power of the United States, and he could not believe the United States Government would disturb his title.

Soon after Boone's emigration to Missouri, the Emperor Napoleon, by treaty with Spain, obtained possession of the whole of the vast region west of the Mississippi and Missouri, then known as Louisiana, and the region was transferred to France. It is a curious fact in the history of Boone passing through such wonderful adventures, that he had been a subject of George II., George III., a citizen of the United States, of the temporary nationality of Transylvania, an adopted son and citizen of the Shawanese tribe of Indians, a subject of Charles IV of Spain, and now he found himself a subject of the first Napoleon, whose empire was then filling the world with its renown.

Not long after this, the Emperor sold the country, as we have recorded, to the United States, saying with that prophetic wisdom which characterised this extraordinary man, "I have now given England a rival upon the seas." The fulfilment of this prophecy has since then been every hour in process of development.

Colonel Boone seems to have been very happy in his new home. He still enjoyed his favorite pursuit of hunting, for the forests around him were filled with game and with animals whose rich furs were every year becoming more valuable. The distinguished naturalist, J. J. Audubon, visited him in his solitary retreat, and spent a night with him. In his Ornithological Biography he gives the following narrative which he received from Boone, that evening as they sat at the cabin fire. We give the story in the words of the narrator:

"Daniel Boone, or as he was usually called in the Western country, Colonel Boone, happened to spend a night with me under the same roof, more than twenty years ago. We had returned from a shooting excursion, in the course of which his extraordinary skill in the management of the rifle had been fully displayed. On retiring to the room appropriated to that remarkable individual and myself for the night, I felt anxious to know more of his exploits and adventures than I did, and accordingly took the liberty of proposing numerous questions to him.

"The stature and general appearance of this wanderer of the western forests approached the gigantic. His chest was broad and prominent, his muscular powers displayed themselves in every limb; his countenance gave indication of his great courage, enterprise and perseverance; and when he spoke the very motion of his lips brought the impression that whatever he uttered could not be otherwise than strictly true. I undressed while he merely took off his hunting shirt and arranged a few folds of blankets on the floor, choosing rather to lie there, as he observed, than on the softest bed. When we had both disposed of ourselves each after his own fashion, he related to me the following account of his powers of memory, which I lay before your kind reader in his own words, hoping that the simplicity of his style may prove interesting to you:

"'I was once,' said he, 'on a hunting expedition on the banks of the Green River, when the lower parts of Kentucky were still in the hands of nature, and none but the sons of the soil were looked upon as its lawful proprietors. We Virginians had for some time been waging a war of intrusion upon them, and I among the rest rambled through the woods in pursuit of their race, as I now would follow the tracks of any ravenous animal. The Indians outwitted me one dark night, and I was as unexpectedly as suddenly made a prisoner by them.

"'The trick had been managed with great skill; for no sooner had I extinguished the fire of my camp, and laid me down to rest in full security, as I thought, than I felt seized by an undistinguishable number of hands, and was immediately pinioned as if about to be led to the scaffold for execution. To have attempted to be refractory would have proved useless and dangerous to my life, and I suffered myself to be removed from my camp to theirs, a few miles distant, without uttering a word of complaint. You are aware, I daresay, that to act in this manner was the best policy, as you understand that by so doing, I proved to the Indians at once that I was born and bred as fearless of death as any of themselves.

"'When we reached the camp great rejoicings were exhibited. Two squaws and a few papooses appeared particularly delighted at the sight of me, and I was assured by every unequivocal gesture and word that on the morrow the mortal enemy of the red skins would cease to live. I never opened my lips, but was busy contriving some scheme which might enable me to give the rascals a slip before dawn. The women immediately fell a searching about my hunting shirt for whatever they might think valuable, and fortunately for me soon found my flask filled with strong whiskey.

"'A terrific grin was exhibited on their murderous countenances, while my heart throbbed with joy at the anticipation of their intoxication. The crew began immediately to beat their bellies and sing, as they passed the bottle from mouth to mouth. How often did I wish the flask ten times its size and filled with *aquafortis*! I observed that the squaws drank more freely than the warriors, and again my spirits were about to be depressed when the report of a gun was heard at a distance. The Indians all jumped on their feet. The singing and drinking were both brought to a stand, and I saw with inexpressible joy the men walk off to some distance and talk to the squaws. I knew that they were consulting about me, and I foresaw that in a few moments the warriors would go to discover the cause of the gun having been fired so near their camp. I expected that the squaws would be left to guard me. Well, sir, it was just so. They returned, the men took up their guns and walked away. The squaws sat down again and in less than five minutes had my bottle up to their dirty mouths, gurgling down their throats the remains of the whiskey.

"'With pleasure did I see them becoming more and more drunk, until the liquor took such hold of them that it was quite impossible for these women to be of any service. They tumbled down, rolled about and began to snore, when I, having no other chance of freeing myself from the cords that fastened me, rolled over and over towards the fire, and after a short time burned them asunder. I rose on my feet, snatched up my rifle, and for once in my life spared that of Indians. I now recollected how desirous I once or twice felt to lay open the skulls of the wretches with my tomahawk. But when I again thought upon killing beings unprepared and unable to defend themselves, it looked like murder without need, and I gave up the idea.

"'But, sir, I felt determined to mark the spot, and walking to a thrifty ash sapling, I cut out of it three large chips and ran off. I soon reached the river, soon crossed it, and threw myself into the cane-brakes, imitating the tracks of an Indian with my feet, so that no chance might be left for those from whom I had escaped to overtake me.

"'It is now nearly twenty years since this happened, and more than five since I left the whites' settlement, which I might never probably have visited again, had I not been called upon as a witness in a law suit which was pending in Kentucky, and which I really believe would never have been settled had I not come forward and established the beginning of a certain boundary line. The story is this, sir:

"'Mr. —— moved from Old Virginia into Kentucky, and having a large tract granted to him in the new State, laid claim to a certain parcel of land adjoining Green River, and, as chance would have it, took for one of his corners the very ash tree on which I had made my mark, beginning, as it is expressed in the deed, 'At an ash marked by three distinct notches of the tomahawk of a white man.'

"'The tree had grown much, and the bark had covered the marks. But somehow or other Mr. —— had heard from someone all that I have already said to you, and thinking that I might remember the spot alluded to in the deed, but which was no longer discoverable, wrote for me to come and try at least to find the place or the tree. His letter mentioned that all my expenses should be paid; and not caring much about once more going back to Kentucky, I started and met Mr. ——. After some conversation, the affair with the Indians came to my recollection. I considered for a while, and began to think that, after all, I could find the very spot, as well as the tree, if it were yet standing.

"Mr. —— and I mounted our horses and off we went to the Green River bottoms. After some difficulty—for you must be aware, sir, that great changes have taken place in those woods—I found at last the spot where I had crossed the river, and waiting for the moon to rise, made for the course in which I thought the ash trees grew. On approaching the place I felt as if the Indians were there still, and as if I were still a prisoner among them. Mr. —— and I camped near what I conceived the spot, and waited until the return of day.

"'At the rising of the sun I was on foot, and after a good deal of musing thought that an ash tree, then in sight, must be the very one on which I had made my mark. I felt as if there could be no doubt about it, and mentioned my thought to Mr. ——.

"'Well, Colonel Boone,' said he, 'if you think so I hope that it may prove true, but we must have some witnesses. Do you stay hereabouts and I will go and bring some of the settlers whom I know.'

"'I agreed. Mr. —— trotted off, and I, to pass the time, rambled about to see if a deer was still living in the land. But ah! sir, what a wonderful difference thirty years makes in a country! Why, at the time when I was caught by the Indians, you would not have walked out in any direction more than a mile without shooting a buck or a bear. There were then thousands of buffaloes on the hills in Kentucky. The land looked as if it never would become poor; and to hunt in those days was a pleasure indeed. But when I was left to myself on the banks of Green River, I daresay for the last time in my life, a few *signs* only of the deer were seen, and as to a deer itself I saw none.

"'Mr. —— returned, accompanied by three gentlemen. They looked upon me as if I had been Washington himself, and walked to the ash tree, which I now called my own, as if in quest of a long lost treasure. I took an axe from one of them and cut a few chips off the bark. Still no signs were to be seen. So I cut again until I thought it time to be cautious, and I scraped and worked away with my butcher knife until I *did* come to where my tomahawk had left an impression on the wood. We now went regularly to work and scraped at the tree with care until three hacks, as plain as any three notches ever were, could be seen. Mr. —— and the other gentlemen were astonished, and I must allow that I was as much surprised as pleased myself. I made affidavit of this remarkable occurrence in presence of these gentlemen. Mr. —— gained his cause. I left Green River forever, and came to where we are now; and, sir, I wish you a good night."

The life of this wonderful man was filled with similar adventures, many of which can now never be recalled. The following narrative will

A New Home

give the reader an idea of the scenes which were continually occurring in those bloody conflicts between the white settlers and the Indians:

"A widow was residing in a lonely log cabin, remote from any settlers, in what is now Bourbon County, Kentucky. Her lonely hut consisted of but two rooms. One, the aged widow occupied herself, with two sons and a widowed daughter with an infant child; the other was tenanted by her three unmarried daughters, the oldest of whom was twenty years of age.

"It was eleven o'clock at night, and the members of the industrious family in their lonely habitation had retired, with the exception of one of the daughters and one of the sons who was keeping her company. Some indications of danger had alarmed the young man, though he kept his fears to himself.

"The cry apparently of owls in an adjoining forest was heard, answering each other in rather an unusual way. The horses in the enclosure by the side of the house, who seemed to have an instinct informing them of the approach of the Indians, seemed much excited and galloped around snorting with terror. Soon steps were heard in the yard, and immediately several loud knocks were made at the door, with someone enquiring, in good English, 'Who keeps this house?' The young man very imprudently was just unbarring the door when the mother sprang from the bed, exclaiming that they were Indians.

"The whole family was immediately aroused, and the young men seized their guns. The Indians now threw off all disguise, and began to thunder at the door, endeavoring to break it down. Through a loop hole prepared for such an emergency, a rifle shot, discharged at the savages, compelled a precipitate retreat. Soon, however, they cautiously returned, and attacking the other end of the cabin, where they found a point not exposed to the fire from within, they succeeded at length in breaking through, and entered the room occupied by the three girls. One of them they seized and bound. Her sister made desperate resistance, and stabbed one of the Indians to the heart with a large knife which she was using at the loom. They immediately tomahawked her and she fell dead upon the floor. The little girl in the gloom of midnight they had overlooked. The poor little thing ran out of the door, and might have escaped had she not, in her terror, lost all self-control, and ran round the house wringing her hands and crying bitterly.

"The brothers, agonized by the cries of their little sister, were just about opening the door to rush out to her rescue, when their more prudent mother declared that the child must be abandoned to its fate, that any attempt to save her would not only be unavailing, but would ensure the certain destruction of them all. Just then the child uttered a most frantic scream. They heard the dull sound as of a tomahawk falling upon the brain. There were a few convulsive moans, and all again was silent. It was but too evident to all what these sounds signified.

"Presently the crackling of flames was heard, and through the port holes could be seen the glare of the rising conflagration, while the shouts of the savages grew more exultant. They had set fire to the end of the building occupied by the daughters. The logs were dry as tinder, and the devouring element was soon enveloping the whole building in its fatal embrace. To remain in the cabin was certain death, in its most appalling form. In rushing out there was a bare possibility that some might escape. There was no time for reflection. The hot stifling flames and smothering smoke were rolling in upon them, when they opened the door and rushed out into the outer air, endeavoring as soon as possible to reach the gloom of the forest.

"The old lady, aided by her eldest son, ran in one direction towards a fence, while the other daughter, with her infant in her arms, accompanied by the younger of the brothers, ran in another direction. The fire was blazing so fiercely as to shed all around the light of day. The old lady had just reached the fence when several rifle balls pierced her body and she fell dead. Her son almost miraculously escaped, and leaping the fence plunged into the forest and disappeared. The other party was pursued by the Indians, with loud yells. Throwing down their guns which they had discharged, the savages rushed upon the young man and his sister with their gleaming tomahawks. Gallantly the brother defended his sister; firing upon the savages as they came rushing on, and then assailing them with the butt of his musket which he wielded with the fury of despair. He fought with such herculean strength as to draw the attention of all the savages upon himself, and thus gave his sister an opportunity of escaping. He soon however fell beneath their tomahawks, and was in the morning found scalped and mangled in the most shocking manner."

Of this family of eight persons two only escaped from this awful scene of midnight massacre. The neighborhood was immediately aroused. The second daughter was carried off a captive by the savages. The fate of the poor girl awakened the deepest sympathy, and by daylight thirty men were assembled on horseback, under the command of Col. Edwards, to pursue the Indians. Fortunately a light snow had fallen during the night. Thus it was impossible for the savages to conceal their trail, and they were followed on the full gallop. The wretches knew full well that they would not be allowed to retire unmolested. They fled with the utmost precipitation, seeking to gain the mountainous region which bordered upon the Licking River.

A hound accompanied the pursuing party. The sagacious animal was very eager in the chase. As the trail became fresh, and the scent indicated that the foe was nearly overtaken, the hound rushing forward, began to bay very loudly. This gave the Indians the alarm. Finding the strength of their captive failing, so that she could no longer continue the rapid flight, they struck their tomahawks into her brain, and left her bleeding and dying upon the snow. Her friends soon came up and found her in the convulsions of death. Her brother sprang from his horse and tried in vain to stop the effusion of blood. She seemed to recognize him, gave him her hand, uttered a few inarticulate words, and died.

The pursuit was then continued with new ardor, and in about twenty minutes the avenging white men came within sight of the savages. With considerable military sagacity, the Indians had taken position upon a steep and narrow ridge, and seemed desirous of magnifying their numbers in the eyes of their pursuers by running from tree to tree and making the forest resound with their hideous yells. The pursuers were, however, too well acquainted with Indian warfare to be deceived by this childish artifice. They dismounted, tied their horses, and endeavored to surround the enemy, so as to cut off his retreat. But the cunning Indians, leaving two of their number behind to delay the pursuit by deceiving the white men into the conviction that they all were there, fled to the mountains. One of this heroic rear-guard—for remaining under the circumstances was the almost certain surrender of themselves to death—was instantly shot. The other, badly wounded, was tracked for a long distance by his blood upon the snow. At length his trail was lost in a running stream. Night came, a dismal night of rain, long and dark. In the morning the snow had melted, every trace of the retreat of the enemy was obliterated, and the further pursuit of the foe was relinquished.

Colonel Boone, deprived of his property by the unrelenting processes of pitiless law, had left Kentucky impoverished and in debt. His rifle was almost the only property he took with him beyond the Mississippi. The rich acres which had been assigned to him there were then of but little more value than so many acres of the sky. Though he was so far away from his creditors that it was almost impossible that they should ever annoy him, still the honest-hearted man was oppressed by the consciousness of his debts, and was very anxious to pay them. The forests were full of game, many of the animals furnishing very valuable furs. He took his rifle, some pack-horses, and, accompanied by a single black servant boy, repaired to the banks of the Osage River to spend the winter in hunting. Here he was taken dangerously sick, and was apprehensive that he should die. We know not what were his religious thoughts upon this occasion, but his calmness in view of death, taken in connection with his blameless, conscientious, and reflective life, and with the fact that subsequently he became an openly avowed disciple of Jesus, indicate that then he found peace in view of pardoned sin through faith in the atonement of Jesus Christ. He pointed out to the black boy the place where, should he die, he wished to be buried. He gave very minute directions in reference to his burial and the disposal f his rifle, blankets, and peltry. Mr. Peck in the following language describes this interesting incident in the life of the pioneer:

> "On another occasion he took pack-horses and went to the country on the Osage river, taking for a camp-keeper a negro boy about twelve or fourteen years of age. Soon after preparing his camp and laying in his supplies for the winter, he was taken sick and lay a long time in camp. The horses were hobbled out on the range. After a period of stormy weather, there came a pleasant and delightful day, and Boone felt able to walk out. With his staff—for he was quite feeble—he took the boy to the

summit of a small eminence and marked out the ground in shape and size of a grave, and then gave the following directions.

"He instructed the boy, in case of his death, to wash and lay his body straight, wrapped up in one of the cleanest blankets. He was then to construct a kind of shovel, and with that instrument and the hatchet to dig a grave exactly as he had marked it out. He was then to drag the body to the place and put it in the grave, which he was directed to cover up, putting posts at the head and foot. Poles were to be placed around and above the surface, the trees to be marked so that the place could be easily found by his friends; the horses were to be caught, the blankets and skins gathered up, with some special instructions about the old rifle, and various messages to his family. All these directions were given, as the boy afterwards declared, with entire calmness, and as if he were giving instructions about ordinary business. He soon recovered, broke up his camp, and returned homeward without the usual signs of a winter's hunt."

One writer says Colonel Boone went on a trapping excursion up the Grand River. This stream rises in the southern part of Iowa, and flows in a southerly course into the Missouri. He was entirely alone. Paddling his canoe up the lonely banks of the Missouri, he entered the Grand River, and established his camp in a silent sheltered cove, where an experienced hunter would with difficulty find it.

Here he first laid in his supply of venison, turkeys, and bear's meat, and then commenced his trapping operation, where no sound of his rifle would disturb the beavers and no smell of gunpowder would excite their alarm. Every morning he took the circuit of his traps, visiting them all in turn. Much to his alarm, he one morning encountered a large encampment of Indians in his vicinity, engaged in hunting. He immediately retreated to his camp and secreted himself. Fortunately for him, quite a deep snow fell that night, which covered his traps. But this same snow prevented him from leaving his camp, lest his footprints should be discovered. For twenty days he continued thus secreted, occasionally, at midnight, venturing to cook a little food, when there was no danger that the smoke of his fire would reveal his retreat. At length the enemy departed, and he was released from his long imprisonment. He subsequently stated that never in his life had he felt so much anxiety for so long a period, lest the Indians should discover his traps and search out his camp.

It seems that the object of Colonel Boone in these long hunting excursions was to obtain furs that he might pay the debts which he still owed in Kentucky. A man of less tender conscience would no longer have troubled himself about them. He was far removed from any importunity on the part of his creditors, or from any annoyance through the law. Still his debts caused him much solicitude, and he could not rest in peace until they were fully paid.

After two or three seasons of this energetic hunting, Colonel Boone succeeded in obtaining a sufficient quantity of furs to enable him, by their sale, to pay all his debts. With this object in view, he set out on his long journey of several hundred miles, through an almost trackless wilderness, to Kentucky. He saw every creditor and paid every dollar. Upon his return, Colonel Boone had just one half dollar in his pocket. But he said triumphantly to his friends who eagerly gathered around him:

> "Now I am ready and willing to die. I am relieved from a burden which has long oppressed me. I have paid all my debts, and no one will say when I am gone, 'Boone was a dishonest man.' I am perfectly willing to die."

In the year 1803, the territory west of the Mississippi came into the possession of the United States. The whole region, embracing what is now Missouri, was then called the territory of Louisiana. Soon after this a commission was appointed, consisting of three able and impartial men, to investigate the validity of the claims to land granted by the action of the Spanish Government. Again poor Boone was caught in the meshes of the law. It was found that he had not occupied the land which had been granted him, that he had not gone to New Orleans to perfect his title, and that his claim was utterly worthless.

"Poor Boone! Seventy-four years old, and the second grasp you have made upon the West has been powerless. You have risked life, and lost the life next dearest your own for the West. In all its fearful forms, death has looked you in the face, and you have moved on to conquer the soil which you did but conquer, that it might be denied to you. You have been the architect of the prosperity of others, but your own crumbles each time as you are about to occupy it. When he lost his farm in Boonesborough, he did not linger around in complainings, but went quietly away, returning only to fulfil the obligations he had incurred. And now this last decision came, even at old age, to leave Daniel Boone, the Pioneer of the West, unable to give a title deed to a solitary acre."[7]

The fur trade was at this time very lucrative. Many who were engaged in it accumulated large fortunes. It was in this traffic that John Jacob Astor laid the foundations of his immense wealth. A guide of Major Long stated that he purchased of an Indian one hundred and twenty beaver skins for two blankets, two gallons of rum, and a pocket mirror. The skins he took to Montreal, where he sold them for over four hundred dollars.

In the employment of the fur companies the trappers are of two kinds, called the "hired hand," and the "free trapper." The former is employed by the month, receiving regular wages, and bringing in all the furs which he can obtain. Be they more or less, he receives his stipulated monthly wages. The free trapper is supplied by the company with traps and certain other conveniences with which he plunges into the forest on his own hook, engaging however to sell to the company, at a stipulated price, whatever furs he may secure.

The outfit of the trapper as he penetrated the vast and trackless region of gloomy forests, treeless prairies, and solitary rivers, spreading everywhere around him, generally consisted of two or three horses, one for the saddle and the others for packs containing his equipment of traps, ammunition, blankets, cooking utensils, etc., in preparation for passing lonely months in the far away solitudes. He would endeavor to find, if possible, a region which neither the white man nor the Indian had ever visited.

The dress of the hunter consisted of a strong shirt of well-dressed and pliant buckskin, ornamented with long fringes. The vanity of dress, if it

---

[7] Life of Boone, by W. H. Bogart, p. 369.

may be so called, followed him into regions where no eye but his own could see its beauties. His pantaloons were also made of buckskin decorated with variously-colored porcupine quills and with long fringes down the outside of the leg. Moccasins, often quite gorgeously embroidered, fitted closely to his feet. A very flexible hat or cap covered his head, generally of felt, obtained from some Indian trader. There was suspended over his left shoulder, so as to hang beneath his right arm, a powder horn and bullet pouch. In the latter he carried balls, flints, steel, and various odds and ends. A long heavy rifle he bore upon his shoulder.

A belt of buckskin buckled tightly around the waist, held a large butcher knife in a sheath of stout buffalo hide, and also a buckskin case containing a whet-stone. A small hatchet or tomahawk was also attached to this belt. Thus rigged and in a new dress the hunter of good proportions presented a very picturesque aspect. With no little pride he exhibited himself at the trading posts, where not only the squaws and the children, but veteran hunters and Indian braves contemplated his person with admiration.

Thus provided the hunter, more frequently alone but sometimes accompanied by two or three others, set out for the mountain streams, as early in the spring as the melting ice would enable him to commence operations against the beaver.

Arrived on his hunting ground he carefully ascends some creek or stream, examining the banks with practiced eye to discern any sign of the presence of beaver or of any other animal whose fur would prove valuable. If a cotton-wood tree lies prostrate he examines it to see if it has been cut down by the sharp tooth of the beaver; and if so whether it has been cut down for food or to furnish material for damming a stream. If the track of a beaver is seen in the mud, he follows the track until he finds a good place to set his steel trap in the run of the animal, hiding it under water and carefully attaching it by a chain to a bush or tree, or to some picket driven into the bank. A float strip is also made fast to the trap, so that should the beaver chance to break away with the trap, this float upon the surface, at the end of a cord a few feet long, would point out the position of the trap.

"When a 'lodge' is discovered the trap is set at the edge of the dam, at the point where the animal passes from deep to shoal water. Early in the morning the hunter always mounts his mule and examines the traps. The captured animals are skinned, and the tails, which are a great dainty, carefully packed into camp. The skin is then stretched over a hoop or frame-work of osier twigs and is allowed to dry, the flesh and fatty substance being carefully scraped off. When dry it is folded into a square sheet, the fur turned inward, and the bundle, containing from about ten to twenty skins, lightly pressed and corded, is ready for transportation.

"During the hunt, regardless of Indian vicinity, the fearless trapper wanders far and near in search of 'sign.' His nerves must ever be in a state of tension and his mind ever present at his call. His eagle eye sweeps around the country, and in an instant detects any foreign appearance. A turned leaf, a blade of grass pressed down, the uneasiness of wild animals, the flight of birds, are all paragraphs to him written in nature's legible hand and plainest language. All the wits of the subtle savage are called into play to gain an advantage over the wily woodsman; but with the instinct of the primitive man, the white hunter has the advantage of a civilised mind, and thus provided seldom fails to outwit, under equal advantages, the cunning savage.

"Sometimes the Indian following on his trail, watches him set his traps on a shrub-belted stream, and passing up the bed, like Bruce of old, so that he may leave no track, he lies in wait in the bushes until the hunter comes to examine. Then waiting until he approaches his ambush within a few feet, whiz flies the home-drawn arrow, never failing at such close quarters to bring the victim to the ground. For one white scalp, however, that dangles in the smoke of an Indian lodge, a dozen black ones at the end of the hunt ornament the camp-fire of the rendezvous.

"At a certain time when the hunt is over, or they have loaded their pack animals, the trappers proceed to their rendezvous, the locality of which has been previously agreed upon; and here the traders and agents of the fur companies await them, with such assortments of goods as their hardy customers may require, including generally a fair supply of alcohol. The trappers drop in singly and in small bands, bringing their packs of beaver to this mountain market, not unfrequently to the value of a thousand dollars each, the produce of one hunt. The dissipation of the rendezvous, however, soon turns the trapper's pocket inside out. The goods brought by the traders, although of the most inferior quality, are sold at enormous prices. Coffee twenty and thirty shillings a pint cup, which is the usual measure; tobacco fetches ten and fifteen shillings a plug; alcohol from twenty to fifty shillings a pint; gunpowder sixteen shillings a pint cup, and all other articles at proportionately exhorbitant prices.

"The rendezvous is one continued scene of drunkenness, gambling, brawling and fighting, so long as the money and credit of the trappers last. Seated Indian fashion around the fires, with a blanket spread before them, groups are seen with their 'decks' of cards playing at 'euchre,' 'poker,' and 'seven-up,' the regular mountain games. The stakes are beaver, which is here current coin; and when the fur is gone, their horses, mules, rifles and shirts, hunting packs and breeches are staked. Daring gamblers make the rounds of the camp, challenging each other to play for the highest stake—his horse, his squaw if he have one, and as once happened his scalp. A trapper often squanders the produce of his hunt, amounting to hundreds of dollars, in a couple of hours; and supplied on credit with another equipment, leaves the rendezvous for another expedition which has the same result, time after time, although one tolerably successful hunt would enable him to return to the settlements and civilised life with an ample sum to purchase and stock a farm, and enjoy himself in ease and comfort for the remainder of his days.

"These annual gatherings are often the scene of bloody duels, for over their cups and cards no men are more quarrelsome than your mountaineers. Rifles at twenty paces settle all differences, and as may be imagined, the fall of one or other of the combatants is certain, or, as sometimes happens, both fall at the same fire."[8]

---

[8] Ruxton's Travels.

Chapter 14

CONCLUSION

Colonel Boone having lost all his property, sent in a memorial, by the advice of his friends, to the Legislature of Kentucky, and also another to Congress. Kentucky was now a wealthy and populous State, and was not at all indisposed to recognise the invaluable services she had received from Colonel Boone. In allusion to these services Governor Moorehead said:

"It is not assuming too much to declare, that without Colonel Boone, in all probability the settlements could not have been upheld; and the conquest of Kentucky might have been reserved for the emigrants of the nineteenth century."

What obstacle stood in the way of a liberal grant of land by the Kentucky Legislature we do not know. We simply know that by a unanimous vote of that body, the following preamble and resolution were passed:

"The Legislature of Kentucky, taking into view the many eminent services rendered by Colonel Boone, in exploring and settling the western country, from which great advantages have resulted, not only to this State, but to this country in general, and that from circumstances over which he had no control, he is now reduced to poverty; not having, so far as appears, an acre of land out of the vast territory he has been a great instrument in peopling; believing also that it is as unjust as it is impolitic, that useful enterprise and eminent services should go unrewarded by a Government where merit confers the only distinction; and having sufficient reason to believe that a grant of ten thousand acres of land, which he claims in Upper Louisiana, would have been confirmed by the Spanish Government, had not said territory passed by cession into the hands of the General Government; therefore

"Resolved by the General Assembly of the Commonwealth of Kentucky: That our Senators in Congress be requested to make use of their exertions to procure a grant of land in said territory to said Boone, either the ten thousand acres to which he appears to have an equitable claim, from the grounds set forth to this Legislature, by way of confirmation, or to such quantity in such place as shall be deemed most advisable by way of donation."

While this question was pending before Congress, Colonel Boone met with the heaviest grief he had thus far encountered on his stormy pilgrimage. In the month of March, 1813, his wife, whom he tenderly loved, died at the age of seventy-six. She had been one of the best of wives and mothers, seeking in all things to conform to the wishes of her husband, and aid him in his plans. She was a devoted wife and a loving mother. Colonel Boone selected upon the summit of a ridge the place for her burial, and marked out the spot for his own grave by her side.

We have no means of knowing what were the religious views which sustained Mrs. Boone in her dying hour. Her life was passed in the discharge of the humble duties of a home in the wilderness, and she had no biographer. But we do know that the religion of Jesus had penetrated many of these remote cabins, and had ennobled the lives of many of these hardy pioneers.

Under the Spanish Government, the Roman Catholic Religion was the established religion of the province, and none other was openly tolerated. Still, the authorities were so anxious to encourage emigration from the United States, that they avoided any rigorous enforcement of the law. Each emigrant was required to be "a good Catholic," *un bon Catholique*. But by connivance of the authorities, only a few general questions were asked, such as:

> "Do you believe in Almighty God? in the Holy Trinity? in the true Apostolic Church? in Jesus Christ our Saviour? in the Holy Evangelists?"

The ceremony was closed by the declaration that the applicant was *un bon Catholique*. Thus many Protestant families entered the Spanish territory, and remained undisturbed in their religious principles. Protestant clergymen crossed over the Mississippi river and, unmolested, preached the gospel in the log cabins of the settlers. The Catholic priests received their salaries from the Spanish crown, and no taxes for religion were imposed.

The Reverend John Clark, a very zealous Christian minister, made monthly excursions to the Spanish territory. The commandant at St. Louis, Mr. Trudeau, would take no notice of his presence till the time when he knew that Mr. Clark was about to leave. Then he would send a threatening message ordering him to leave within three days. One of the emigrants, Mr. Murich, of the Baptist persuasion, who knew the commandant very well, petitioned for permission to hold religious meetings at his house and to have Mr. Clark preach. Mr. Trudeau replied:

> "You must not put a bill upon your house, or call it a church. But if any of your friends choose to meet at your house, sing, pray, and talk about religion, you will not be molested provided you continue, as I suppose you are, *un bon Catholique*."

Thus, in reality, there was scarcely any restraint in those remote regions, even under the Spanish regime, imposed upon religious freedom. Christian songs, the penitential and the triumphant, often ascended, blended with prayers and praises from these lonely and lowly homes in the wilderness. Thus characters were formed for heaven, and life was ennobled, and often far more of true nobility of soul and more real and satisfying enjoyment were found in those log huts, illumined only by the blaze of the pitch pine knot, than Louis XIV. and his courtiers ever experienced amidst the splendors and the luxuries of Versailles and of Marly.

We do not know that Colonel Boone ever made a public profession of his faith in Christ, though somewhere we have seen it stated that he died an honored member of the Methodist Church. It is certain that the religious element predominated in his nature. He was a thoughtful, serious, devout, good man. He walked faithfully in accordance with the light and the privileges which were conferred upon him in his singularly adventurous life.

Colonel Boone was seventy-nine years of age when Congress conferred upon him a grant of eight hundred and fifty acres of land. He had never repined at his lot, had never wasted his breath in unavailing murmurs. He contentedly took life as it came, and was ever serene and cheerful. But this grant of land, though it came so late, greatly cheered him. He was no longer dependent upon others. He had property rapidly increasing in value to leave to the children and the grand-children he so tenderly loved. His aged limbs would no longer allow him to expose himself to the vicissitudes of hunting, and he took up his abode with one of his sons, enjoying, perhaps, as serene and happy an old age as ever fell to the lot of mortals. His conversation often gathered charmed listeners around him, for he had a very retentive memory, and his mind was crowded with the incidents of his romantic career. It is said that at this period of his life an irritable expression never escaped his lips. His grand-children vied with each other in affectionate attentions to one whom they ardently loved, and of whose celebrity they were justly proud.

Colonel Galloway, the gentleman whose two daughters were captured, with one of the daughters of Colonel Boone, in a boat by the Indians, which event our readers will recall to mind, visited Colonel Boone in Missouri about this time. He gives a very pleasing description of the gentle and genial old man, as he then found him.

His personal appearance was venerable and attractive, very neatly clad in garments spun, woven, and made in the cabin. His own room consisted of a cabin by itself, and was in perfect order. "His countenance was pleasant, calm, and fair, his forehead high and bold, and the soft silver of his hair in unison with his length of days. He spoke feelingly and with solemnity of being a creature of Providence, ordained by heaven as a pioneer in the wilderness to advance the civilization and the extension of his country. He professed the belief that the Almighty had assigned to him a work to perform, and that he had only followed the pathway of duty in the work he had pursued; that he had discharged his duty to God and his country by following the direction of Providence." His stormy day of life had passed away into an evening of unusual beauty and serenity.

Still he was continually busy, engaged in innumerable acts of kindness for his neighbors and his friends. He could repair rifles, make and carve powder horns of great beauty, and could fashion moccasins and snowshoes of the most approved patterns. His love for the solitude of the wilderness, and for the excitement of the hunter's life, continued unabated to the last. He loved to cut tender slices of venison, and to toast them upon the end of his ramrod over the glaring coals of his cabin fire, finding in that repast a treat more delicious than any gourmand ever yet experienced in the viands of the most costly restaurants of the Palais Royal, or the Boulevard.

Upon one occasion he could not resist the impulse of again going hunting, though in the eighty-second year of his age. Exacting from his friends the promise that should he die, his remains should be brought back and buried by the side of those of his wife, he took a boy with him and went to the mouth of the Kansas River, where he remained two weeks.

Returning from this, his last expedition, he visited his youngest son, Major Nathan Boone, who had reared a comfortable stone house in that remote region, to which emigrants were now rapidly moving. Here he died after an illness of but three days, on the 26th day of September, 1820. He was then eighty-six years of age.

Soon after the death of his wife, Colonel Boone made his own coffin, which he kept under his bed awaiting the day of his burial. In this coffin he was buried by the side of his wife. Missouri, though very different from the Missouri of the present day, was no longer an unpeopled wilderness. The Indians had retired; thousands of emigrants had flocked to its fertile plains, and many thriving settlements had sprung up along the banks of its magnificent streams. The great respect with which Colonel Boone was regarded by his fellow-citizens, was manifest in the large numbers who were assembled at his burial. The Legislature of Missouri, which chanced then to be in session, adjourned for one day, in respect for his memory, and passed a resolve that all the members should wear a badge of mourning for twenty days. This was the first Legislature of the new State.

Colonel Boone was the father of nine children, five sons and four daughters. His two eldest sons were killed by the Indians. His third son, Daniel Morgan Boone, had preceded his father in his emigration to the Upper Louisiana, as it was then called, and had taken up his residence in the Femme Osage settlement. He became a man of influence and comparative wealth, and attained the advanced age of fourscore. Jesse, the fourth son, also emigrated to Upper Louisiana about the year 1806, where he died a few years after. The youngest son, Nathan, whose privilege it was to close his father's eyes in death, had found a home beyond the Mississippi; he became a man of considerable note, and received the commission of Captain in the United States Dragoons. The daughters, three of whom married, lived and died in Kentucky.

In the meantime Kentucky, which Boone had found a pathless wilderness, the hunting ground of Indians who were scarcely less wild and savage than the beasts they pursued in the chase, was rapidly becoming one of the most populous, wealthy and prosperous States in the Union. Upon the eastern bank of the Kentucky River, the beautiful city of Frankfort had risen surrounded by remarkably romantic and splendid scenery. It had become the capital of the State, and was situated about sixty miles from the entrance of the Kentucky into the Ohio River. Many of the houses were tastefully built of brick or of marble, and the place was noted for its polished, intelligent, and hospitable society.

It was but a few miles above Frankfort upon this same river that Colonel Boone had reared the log fort of Boonesborough, when scarcely a white man could be found west of the Alleghanies. In the year 1845, the citizens of Frankfort, having, in accordance with the refinements of modern tastes, prepared a beautiful rural cemetery in the suburbs of their town, resolved to consecrate it by the interment of the remains of Daniel Boone and his wife. The Legislature, appreciating the immense obligations of the State to the illustrious pioneer, co-operated with the citizens of Frankfort in this movement. For twenty-five years the remains of Col. Boone and his wife had been mouldering in the grave upon the banks of the Missouri.

"There seemed," said one of the writers of that day, "to be a peculiar propriety in this testimonial of the veneration borne by the Commonwealth for the memory of its illustrious dead. And it was fitting that the soil of Kentucky should afford the final resting place for his remains, whose blood in life had been so often shed to protect it from the fury of savage hostility. It was the beautiful and touching manifestation of filial affection shown by children to the memory of a beloved parent; and it was right that the generation which was reaping the fruits of his toils and dangers should desire to have in their midst and decorate with the tokens of their love, the sepulchre of this Primeval Patriarch whose stout heart watched by the cradle of this now powerful Commonwealth."

The honored remains of Daniel Boone and his wife were brought from Missouri to Frankfort, and the re-interment took place on the 13th of September, 1845. The funeral ceremonies were very imposing. Colonel Richard M. Johnson, who had been Vice-President of the United States, and others of the most distinguished citizens of Kentucky, officiated as pall-bearers. The two coffins were garlanded with flowers, and an immense procession followed them to their final resting place. The Hon. John J. Crittenden, who was regarded as the most eloquent man in the State, pronounced the funeral oration. And there beneath an appropriate monument, the body of Daniel Boone now lies, awaiting the summons of the resurrection trumpet.

"Life's labor done, securely laid
In this his last retreat,
Unheeded o'er his silent dust,
The storms of earth shall beat."

INDEX

A

age, ix, 19, 21, 25, 29, 33, 77, 86, 90, 117, 127, 165, 169, 181, 184, 192, 194, 195, 196
agriculture, 15
Alleghanies, v, 15, 26, 49, 149, 196
Alleghany, 12, 15, 26, 61, 168, 170, 172
Alleghany mountains, 12, 15, 26, 61, 170
anxiety, 1, 89, 116, 118, 186
assault, 65, 92, 111, 118, 153, 170
authorities, 18, 138, 143, 157, 166, 170, 175, 192

B

backwoodsman, xiii, 35
banks, 8, 10, 11, 18, 21, 22, 23, 26, 31, 37, 39, 40, 41, 44, 49, 52, 54, 63, 64, 74, 82, 91, 92, 93, 101, 102, 118, 125, 128, 130, 137, 139, 140, 143, 148, 149, 154, 158, 163, 167, 172, 173, 176, 177, 180, 184, 185, 188, 195, 197
birds, 6, 22, 33, 54, 99, 189
bleeding, 95, 107, 140, 183
blood, 5, 11, 64, 65, 83, 103, 107, 115, 128, 140, 159, 183, 184, 197
boat, 34, 44, 102, 128, 149, 153, 163, 164, 165, 172, 176, 194
bones, 150, 155
Boone, Daniel, v, xiii, 16, 17, 22, 23, 24, 26, 27, 28, 36, 50, 51, 53, 54, 59, 67, 68, 70, 71, 72, 73, 74, 77, 80, 87, 89, 93, 94, 95, 96, 97, 109, 127, 135, 136, 143, 148, 158, 167, 171, 177, 187, 196, 197
brain, 5, 56, 87, 125, 182, 183
breathing, 63, 103, 117
brothers, 19, 88, 93, 114, 136, 182
buffalo, 21, 22, 24, 49, 51, 52, 54, 56, 77, 91, 132, 136, 137, 139, 140, 148, 188

C

Caribbean Sea, 2
cattle, 64, 79, 95, 120, 124, 148, 159, 163
Charleston, 12
Cherokee nation, 13
Cherokees, 13, 15, 65, 138, 154
children, 4, 5, 7, 8, 10, 11, 18, 19, 20, 21, 25, 27, 31, 52, 64, 66, 68, 74, 83, 91, 93, 94, 116, 118, 123, 125, 129, 130, 143,

149, 150, 154, 155, 168, 188, 194, 196, 197
cities, 14, 34, 92, 99
citizens, 46, 85, 126, 196, 197
citizenship, 172
civilization, 7, 9, 12, 23, 34, 52, 58, 74, 93, 124, 157, 167, 169, 170, 195
climate, 6, 7, 13, 18, 55, 57, 75
clothing, 26, 33, 35, 51, 59, 63, 83, 88, 100
Columbus, 1, 2
conflict, 63, 65, 107, 109, 130, 140, 141, 151, 161, 163
construction, 24, 35, 71, 72, 88, 163
conviction, 130, 164, 183
cotton, 35, 53, 103, 104, 188
creditors, 184, 186
creep, 106, 110, 162
critical period, 119
crown, 114, 172, 175, 193
Cumberland Gap, 15, 49, 95

D

danger, 11, 12, 19, 20, 27, 34, 36, 53, 61, 74, 77, 79, 81, 90, 97, 110, 116, 132, 135, 149, 151, 161, 181, 185
despair, 56, 84, 111, 163, 182
destruction, 15, 93, 96, 97, 102, 120, 138, 140, 141, 150, 153, 156, 182
dignity, 67, 69, 90, 155, 157
disappointment, 7, 118, 130
disaster, 44, 95, 141, 143
distress, 127, 149

E

emergency, 89, 181
emigration, 12, 24, 27, 50, 69, 74, 75, 77, 93, 94, 126, 136, 169, 171, 172, 176, 192, 196
employment, 33, 35, 88, 187

England, 6, 7, 10, 12, 15, 18, 19, 44, 47, 122, 144, 176
Europe, 5, 13, 27, 47
exposure, 18, 34, 53, 115, 146, 148, 153, 157

F

families, 7, 10, 18, 27, 35, 52, 60, 66, 74, 94, 126, 131, 163, 172, 193
fear, xiii, 7, 20, 27, 41, 51, 52, 64, 90, 95, 106, 107, 128, 148, 170, 172
feelings, 2, 14, 159, 168, 171
fertility, 13, 50, 91, 101, 149
flight, 49, 56, 57, 82, 106, 117, 118, 130, 141, 151, 162, 163, 183, 189
food, 31, 36, 55, 59, 84, 87, 88, 97, 111, 114, 137, 143, 169, 170, 171, 185, 188
foundations, xiii, 187
France, 3, 19, 39, 42, 44, 45, 46, 101, 176
freedom, 58, 59, 90, 95, 193
friendship, 60, 114, 123, 155

G

gambling, 190
God, 1, 2, 5, 41, 50, 80, 117, 155, 156, 193, 195
grass, 3, 4, 24, 91, 99, 106, 139, 144, 189
growth, 6, 7, 8, 25, 103
guilty, 18, 147
gunpowder, 10, 33, 185, 190

H

hair, 33, 59, 82, 87, 100, 110, 114, 195
happiness, 19, 23, 31, 36, 41, 50, 60, 90, 113, 118, 158
health, 36, 55, 69, 90, 93, 110
height, 24, 29, 30, 52, 90, 101, 144

Index

heroism, 50, 97, 125, 150, 165
history, xiv, 39, 80, 117, 125, 128, 141, 176
homes, 12, 32, 50, 64, 66, 122, 126, 130, 143, 144, 149, 157, 163, 168, 193
horses, 3, 13, 21, 27, 35, 51, 71, 75, 76, 81, 82, 83, 89, 91, 93, 94, 111, 119, 120, 148, 152, 153, 154, 155, 159, 168, 179, 181, 183, 184, 185, 187, 190
hostility, 6, 10, 71, 102, 197
human, 10, 22, 24, 32, 36, 42, 49, 63, 64, 113
human nature, 10
hunting, 12, 14, 20, 21, 23, 30, 33, 34, 35, 37, 40, 41, 50, 53, 54, 68, 69, 71, 87, 88, 92, 96, 97, 107, 110, 112, 114, 122, 131, 147, 152, 155, 158, 169, 176, 177, 178, 184, 185, 186, 188, 190, 194, 195, 196
husband, 22, 50, 52, 90, 108, 168, 192

I

imagination, 28, 90, 91, 99, 100
imprisonment, 185
Indian warfare, v, 61, 64, 65, 67, 73, 125, 183
Indians, xiii, 5, 6, 7, 9, 10, 11, 12, 13, 14, 15, 16, 17, 18, 19, 23, 26, 28, 33, 35, 40, 41, 42, 43, 44, 49, 50, 51, 54, 55, 56, 57, 58, 59, 61, 62, 63, 64, 65, 66, 67, 68, 70, 71, 72, 73, 74, 77, 78, 79, 80, 81, 82, 83, 84, 85, 87, 88, 91, 92, 93, 96, 97, 101, 102, 103, 104, 105, 106, 107, 108, 109, 110, 111, 112, 113, 114, 115, 116, 117, 118, 119, 121, 122, 123, 124, 125, 128, 129, 130, 131, 132, 135, 136, 137, 138, 139, 140, 141, 142, 143, 144, 145, 146, 147, 148, 149, 150, 151, 152, 153, 154, 155, 156, 157, 158, 159, 161, 162, 163, 164, 165, 166, 170, 172, 176, 177, 178, 179, 180, 181, 182, 183, 194, 195, 196

industry, 9, 55, 124, 148
inmates, 4, 17, 19, 111, 116, 129, 147, 151, 161
instinct, 20, 27, 57, 97, 133, 181, 189
intelligence, 12, 67, 81, 113, 118, 119, 121, 123, 139, 147

J

jurisdiction, 136

K

Kentucky, v, xiii, 15, 16, 34, 36, 37, 49, 52, 55, 61, 69, 70, 71, 72, 74, 76, 81, 90, 92, 93, 96, 97, 115, 124, 125, 126, 128, 130, 135, 136, 138, 141, 143, 144, 147, 148, 149, 150, 152, 154, 155, 156, 157, 158, 159, 163, 164, 165, 167, 168, 169, 170, 171, 172, 177, 179, 180, 181, 184, 186, 191, 192, 196, 197

L

lakes, 7, 28, 42, 53, 59
Laurel Mountain, 16
leadership, 15, 129, 139
liberty, 5, 10, 46, 59, 85, 114, 177
light, 2, 4, 30, 37, 38, 41, 57, 127, 142, 164, 182, 183, 194
London, 8, 13, 15
Louisiana, v, 39, 44, 45, 46, 100, 170, 176, 186, 192, 196
love, 8, 15, 20, 23, 31, 32, 50, 63, 91, 154, 155, 195, 197
lying, 42, 106, 132, 137

M

meat, 5, 26, 30, 63, 100, 112, 185

memory, 18, 32, 42, 43, 98, 177, 194, 196, 197
Miami, 83, 112, 113, 115, 116, 128, 129, 130, 138, 143
military, 12, 65, 67, 79, 118, 129, 136, 143, 144, 175, 183
murder, 7, 14, 78, 179

N

natural resources, 47
North America, 3, 5, 6, 8, 17
North Carolina, 6, 16, 19, 21, 50, 52, 69, 80, 118, 125, 128, 167, 169, 172

O

Ohio, 12, 13, 31, 41, 61, 62, 63, 64, 65, 67, 68, 69, 70, 76, 81, 83, 84, 86, 90, 91, 92, 96, 97, 98, 118, 119, 128, 130, 132, 136, 137, 139, 143, 148, 149, 150, 153, 154, 155, 156, 163, 168, 172, 196

P

peace, 14, 15, 41, 49, 63, 64, 67, 68, 93, 96, 147, 153, 154, 155, 156, 166, 172, 176, 184, 186
pioneers, v, 31, 36, 71, 73, 74, 75, 76, 79, 80, 91, 94, 96, 123, 125, 132, 136, 137, 139, 140, 144, 147, 156, 158, 166, 169, 170, 175, 192
Pittsburg, 13, 169
pleasure, 11, 58, 60, 83, 90, 178, 180
population, 24, 31, 41, 171
preparation, iv, 35, 62, 80, 83, 93, 96, 117, 187
prisoners, 55, 56, 57, 78, 81, 112, 123, 130, 131, 141, 154, 155, 166
prosperity, 8, 15, 56, 64, 93, 95, 187

protection, 2, 8, 11, 12, 20, 79, 87, 100, 119, 129, 130, 156

R

religion, 192, 193
reputation, 5, 67, 111, 126, 127
resistance, 55, 111, 130, 152, 153, 181
resolution, 93, 157, 191
resources, 21, 58, 79, 84, 113, 144, 156, 159
risk, 45, 77, 85, 93, 142

S

safety, 15, 61, 65, 74, 82, 88, 93, 100, 104, 106, 108, 118, 135, 136, 163, 171
security, 36, 73, 75, 118, 148, 177
services, iv, 67, 96, 141, 167, 171, 191
settlements, 3, 12, 14, 15, 17, 21, 34, 41, 57, 59, 61, 63, 66, 67, 69, 75, 80, 81, 84, 93, 97, 98, 99, 125, 129, 130, 131, 132, 135, 138, 139, 141, 143, 148, 154, 156, 163, 190, 191, 195
Shawnees, 16
shelter, 22, 51, 66, 94, 144
shoot, 37, 68, 78, 97, 102, 118, 140, 147, 152, 162
shores, 17, 40, 44, 69, 164
signs, 49, 53, 110, 111, 139, 153, 180, 185
society, xiii, 11, 19, 27, 34, 36, 99, 100, 136, 147, 149, 159, 196
solitude, 12, 17, 19, 20, 23, 24, 26, 32, 40, 98, 99, 113, 158, 169, 172, 195
South America, 3
South Carolina, 3, 12, 13
Spain, 1, 3, 7, 19, 39, 44, 45, 46, 170, 172, 176
speech, 63, 67, 75, 115, 123, 154, 156
starvation, 85, 115, 117
storms, 21, 88, 158, 197
sympathy, 113, 114, 183

T

tall trees, 29
Tennessee, 14, 15, 34, 35, 91, 96, 138
territory, 8, 18, 46, 47, 50, 54, 70, 131, 175, 186, 192, 193
tobacco, 10, 144, 146, 155, 190
torture, 9, 83, 102, 112, 123, 144, 149, 166
trade, 42, 43, 46, 187
treatment, 4, 70, 111, 112, 114, 168, 170

U

United States, 34, 39, 44, 45, 46, 47, 141, 176, 186, 192, 196, 197

V

vegetables, 18, 23, 26, 98
victims, 11, 95, 122, 123, 131, 137
violence, 125, 150, 166
Virginia, 6, 8, 12, 13, 15, 28, 61, 63, 64, 76, 80, 96, 98, 126, 135, 136, 141, 150, 156, 157, 158, 168, 172, 179

W

Walker, Doctor Thomas, 15
war, 7, 9, 11, 14, 15, 17, 43, 44, 45, 46, 49, 62, 63, 64, 68, 75, 79, 86, 87, 95, 96, 103, 111, 116, 119, 122, 124, 126, 128, 129, 131, 137, 138, 139, 144, 147, 148, 151, 154, 157, 166, 172, 177
water, 42, 43, 72, 74, 77, 84, 90, 104, 110, 118, 124, 141, 153, 170, 188, 189
wealth, 5, 6, 8, 12, 36, 43, 68, 113, 187, 196
weapons, 11, 65, 80, 130
wild animals, 137, 189
wilderness, v, 5, 7, 11, 12, 15, 17, 20, 21, 22, 23, 24, 25, 26, 27, 28, 31, 34, 40, 42, 44, 50, 51, 53, 57, 58, 59, 60, 61, 65, 70, 74, 75, 80, 81, 85, 87, 88, 93, 94, 95, 96, 97, 98, 99, 100, 102, 110, 113, 115, 117, 118, 122, 125, 128, 136, 137, 146, 147, 150, 151, 153, 156, 159, 168, 170, 171, 172, 176, 186, 192, 193, 195, 196
windows, 4, 30, 58
wood, 1, 21, 24, 32, 103, 104, 117, 118, 151, 180, 188
woodland, 162

Related Nova Publications

LOUIS XIV. MAKERS OF HISTORY SERIES

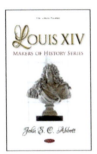

AUTHOR: John S. C. Abbott

SERIES: Historical Figures

BOOK DESCRIPTION: Though this historic sketch contains allusions to all the most important events in the reign of Louis XIV., it has been the main object of the writer to develop the inner life of the palace; to lead the reader into the interior of the Louvre, the Tuileries, Versailles, and Marly, and to exhibit the monarch as a man, in the details of domestic privacy.

HARDCOVER ISBN: 978-1-53615-940-0
RETAIL PRICE: $195

DAVID CROCKETT: HIS LIFE AND ADVENTURES

AUTHOR: John S. C. Abbott

SERIES: Historical Figures

BOOK DESCRIPTION: David Crockett certainly was not a model man. But he was a representative man. He has exerted a very powerful influence over our history. His wild and wondrous life is worthy of the study of every patriot.

HARDCOVER ISBN: 978-1-53615-938-7
RETAIL PRICE: $160

To see a complete list of Nova publications, please visit our website at www.novapublishers.com

Related Nova Publications

THE EARLY LIFE OF ABRAHAM LINCOLN

AUTHOR: Ida M. Tarbell

SERIES: Historical Figures

BOOK DESCRIPTION: *The Early Life of Abraham Lincoln* gets to the heart of young Lincoln's life and the origins of his reputation as "honest Abe." This biography is full of fantastic insights into Lincoln's life: looking not just at the plain facts but also into the character of Abraham Lincoln as a young man.

HARDCOVER ISBN: 978-1-53615-965-3
RETAIL PRICE: $195

To see a complete list of Nova publications, please visit our website at www.novapublishers.com